Indian English Literature

VOLUME 1

Edited by
Basavaraj Naikar

ATLANTIC
PUBLISHERS & DISTRIBUTORS (P) LTD

Published by

ATLANTIC

PUBLISHERS & DISTRIBUTORS (P) LTD

7/22, Ansari Road, Darya Ganj, New Delhi-110002
Phones : +91-11-40775252, 40775214, 23273880, 23275880
Fax : +91-11-23285873
Web : www.atlanticbooks.com
E-mail : orders@atlanticbooks.com

Branch Office: Chennai
Phones : +91-44-48531784, 28291383
E-mail : chennai@atlanticbooks.com

Printed & bound in India by Atlantic Print Services

PREFACE

Indian English literature has been growing slowly and steadily in the twentieth century thereby attracting the critical attention of diligent academicians all over the world. It has gathered a tempo especially in the last two decades of the twentieth century because of the awakening of creative writers in India and abroad rightly encouraged by many national and international awards. Similarly new critical trends like structuralism, post-structuralism, post-modernism, post-colonialism and new historicism etc., have extended the frontiers of understanding and interpretation of literature. While the Indian critic cannot swear by any particular critical school, he has to synthesise many of these schools of thought in his eclectic approach. The old writers like G.V. Desani, Mulk Raj Anand and Raja Rao may be understood and interpreted from new critical perspectives, whereas the new writers may be understood and interpreted from old as well as new perspectives. G.V. Desani's *All About H. Hatterr* may be said to be the first Indian English novel which is known for its stream of consciousness technique, containing the seeds of magical realism and portraying the hybridity and inbetweenity of human experience necessitated by the colonial situation. Similarly Mulk Raj Anand, Raja Rao and Chaman Nahal may be studied from new angles. Women writers from Anita Desai to Arundhati Roy have extended the frontiers of feminine creativity. Likewise there are also many writers who have been unduly neglected by critics because of lack of right kind of publicity and advertisement. Hence, an attempt has been made in this anthology to highlight the old as well as the new; the established as well as the neglected and upcoming writers in order to offer a broader perspective of Indian English literature.

Basavaraj Naikar highlights the variegated allegorical and symbolic element in G.V. Desani's *All About H. Hatterr* ranging from the secular to the religious and from the psychological to the yogic. Binod Mishra offers an elaborate picture of the identity crises undergone by the protagonists of Mulk Raj Anand's novels. Far from harping on the stereotyped themes of social evils, he concentrates on the relatively neglected aspect of psycho-spiritual transformation of characters thereby bringing a freshness into the reading of Anand's novels. Ramesh Kumar Gupta discusses Raja Rao's *The Serpent and the Rope* as a fictional expression of his ontological awareness of Reality supported by the monistic philosophy of Sankara. Basavaraj Naikar discusses the traumatic experience of displacement and anxiety of relocation undergone by Lala Kanshi Ram and his family in *Azadi* which was caused by the partition of the country into India and Pakistan. He points out how the psychological partition between Hindus and Muslims was more horrifying than the political partition between India and Pakistan. G.A. Ghanshyam analyses the deep sense of disillusionment felt by Billy Biswas in the modern materialistic civilization of India and seeking refuge in the primitive world of tribals thereby achieving a sort of mystic union with Nature, which is equivalent to God. Shankar Prasad Singha offers a very perceptive analysis of Basavaraj Naikar's short stories by highlighting the native element, contemporary consciousness and technical experimentation in them. Aroonima Sinha analyses the women characters in Basavaraj Naikar's short stories. She points out how most of the women characters in these stories suffer silently thereby conforming to the expectations of patriarchal society of India. She sees many similarities between the stories of Naikar and R.K. Narayan and Gathas. P.D. Dubbe traces the post-colonial discourse in Amitav Ghosh's *Shadow Lines* and shows how there is no clear demarcation between past and present or between going and coming in human experience.

Asha Choubey offers a detailed analysis of Sonali Ranade's character and shows how Sonali in Nayantara Sahgal's *Rich Like*

Us becomes a truly emancipated woman of the new millenium. Basavaraj Naikar analyses the theme of marital disharmony in Antia Desai's *Cry, the Peacock* and *Where Shall We Go This Summer*? which is aggravated by human abnormality as well as by the absurd situations of life. S.N. Vikram Raj Urs offers a comparative study of Anita Desai's Sita and Margaret Atwood's nameless narrator and shows how both of them discover their self through the interior journey. Asha Choubey analyses Anita Desai's *Fasting, Feasting* from a feminist perspective and shows how the women characters like Uma and Anamika suffer silently because of the power politics of patriarchal society and Hindu fatalism. Basavaraj Naikar analyses the nine stories of Anita Desai collected in her *Diamond Dust* and highlights her feminist perspective, picturesque and poetic descriptions and psychological approach to life. N.B. Masal shows how Shashi Deshpande explores the inner psyche of middle-class women in her novels in a very authentic manner. He draws our attention to the silent suffering of women like Kalyani and Sumi caused by men. Kuldeep Kumar and Gajendra Kumar offer a deconstructionist interpretation of Namita Gokhale's *Paro* whose eponymous heroine tries to achieve her identity by breaking the patriarchal norms of femininity like docility, chastity and submissiveness. He opines that Paro is neither a 'bad' woman nor a 'good' woman but just a 'woman.' Asha Choubey highlights the magical and poetic effect of Arundhati Roy's experimentation with English language and the feminist perspective woven into her artistic vision.

Basavaraj Naikar argues that Girish Karnad's *Tughlaq* is more an experimenter than a tragic figure. Mukesh Ranjan Verma shows how Girish Karnad employs the myth of Yavakri and Paravasu from the *Mahabharata* and dramatizes it with minor changes in the relationships between characters and their motives in order to highlight the futility of knowledge without love and compassion.

M.A. Nare shows how Jayant Mahapatra's wounded Christian psyche helps him understand the suffering of humanity and how he is rooted in the soil and culture of Orissa. Basavaraj Naikar analyses the satirical element in T.R. Rajasekharaiah's poetry (contained in *Desert Blooms*) with appropriate examples and compares it with that of Ezekiel, Shiv K. Kumar and Mahapatra.

The critical insights expressed in these articles will, no doubt, heighten our awareness of the literary beauty of the Indian English poets, dramatists and novelists.

BASAVARAJ NAIKAR
Editor

CONTENTS

1

Allegory and Symbolism in *All About H. Hatterr*

—Basavaraj Naikar

THERE IS, perhaps, no novel in Indian English Literature more puzzling than G.V. Desani's *All About H. Hatterr.* It has teased many a critic because of its grotesque-cum-comic theme as well as its peculiar technique, made all the more complex by the element of allegory and multiple symbolism interwoven in its texture. The novel, thus, has many aspects to be critically explored and interpreted. An attempt, therefore, has been made in the present article to interpret the meaning of allegorical and symbolic element in the novel.

Although both allegorical and symbolic elements are found in the novel, the latter is preponderant as compared to the former which appears to be quite negligible. As far as symbolism is concerned, it may be observed that it is of three kinds : Freudian (psychological), numerological (religious or philosophical) and secular (or general). Many times these symbols are found to be interwoven into one another thereby adding to the complexity and multidimensionality of symbolism a detailed analysis of which may be seen in the following paragraphs.

The first thing that strikes us as symbolic in the novel is the very name of eponymous hero *i.e.* H. Hatterr. The forlorn boy has been adopted by the English Missionary Society. As he finds out that his temperament is not suited to the evangelical life, he escapes from thereafter stealing three books. Now he assumes the nom de plume *i.e.* Hindusthaniwalla Hatterr which is very suggestive and symbolic. The name 'Hatterr' is indicative of his hat which is too large for him and suggests his Anglo-Indian background (and of his adopted parents as well). The hat may be interpreted in terms of Freudian symbolism. The hat can be a symbol of both masculine (in its normal position on the head) and feminine (when upturned) principles. Sigmund Freud opines that "An instance of an obscure symbol of this kind is the *hat* or perhaps head-coverings in general; this usually has a masculine significance, though occasionally a feminine one."[1] But in the present context of the novel, his hat may be taken to symbolise his male ego and his desire to achieve some status (especially that of a sahib in a colonised country) in life. But the story of symbolism of his hat does not end here. The surname 'Hatterr' is prefixed with another word 'Hindusthaniwalla' which adds a new meaning to it. So the long form of his name 'Hindustaniwalla Hatterr' is comically suggestive of the cultural hybridisation of his identity. H. Hatterr has in his blood both the elements of East and West; the coloniser and the colonised; the Hindu and the Christian. His entire life happens to be a struggle to harmonise the two apparently contradictory cultures. His name is obviously a symbol of the encounter between East and West which appears to be a bit comic and even absurd.

The three books that Hatterr has stolen from the Missionary society can be interpreted as general symbols of knowledge or wisdom that he is in quest of. These books easily bring to our mind Prospero's book and holy books or scriptures of organised religions of the world in general. Although he has escaped from the Missionary Society, these books act as vestiges of his erstwhile evangelical life at a theoretical level. The meaning of his future life lies in the actualisation of the theoretical possibilities symbolised by the books. The words of the books are to be translated into a world of experience.

As Hatterr is not formally educated in school or college, he wants to gather his knowledge through the University of *Life*. His desire to meet the seven saints of different parts of India may be interpreted in terms of numerological symbolism. Number 7 happens to be a holy number in both Eastern and Western astrology as well as religion. "Seven is a sacred number in many traditions. Because it is, according to Hippocrates of Chios, related to the lunar phases, seven influences all sublunar things. It appears in the periodicity of chemical elements and of music, and it has generally been connected with the phases of human development to a Grand Climacterium of sixty-three (7×9). Seven is the first prime number of symbolic meaning : it is 'virgin', since it does not generate by multiplication any number under ten, and it is the only integer of the first decade that is not a divisor of 360. Consisting of the spiritual ternary and the practical quaternary (3+4), seven embraces everything created."[2] Heptatic division happens to be accepted as holy and connected with many astrological and cosmic phenomena. For example, seven planets, seven days a week, seven tunes in music, seven days of creation (Christianity), seven worlds, spheres, gates, steps, valleys or veils; seven pillars of wisdom are universally known. Seven is connected with the Hindu fire-god Agni. In folk-tales seven is accepted as a round number and whatever is done seven times is said to be especially effective. In Islamic and Christian legends seven feminine saints and seven masculine saints are commonly mentioned. Number seven happens to be accepted even in modern secular life, especially airplanes bearing the numerals like 707, and 747 etc. The galaxy of seven saints or *saptarṣi maṇḍala* is an important ingredient of the Hindu astrology. In the light of the universally accepted richness of numerological symbolism of 'seven', Hatterr's encounter with the seven saints (however fake they may be) of India is indicative of his quest for spiritual knowledge, experience, holiness and perfection. According to Hindu philosophy every spiritual aspirant has to be guided by his *guru* along the path of salvation. His experiences in life are guided by his *guru* who happens to be the medium of spiritual realisation. Sometimes *guru* is said to be even greater than God himself, as he happens to be a living incarnation of the abstract and invisible principle of Divinity. There is simply no possibility of the attainment of *mokṣa* or salvation without the help of a *guru*. Hatterr's encounter with the seven saints happens to be in line with the Hindu spiritual tradition.

Dreams are quite common in the novel. "Dreams are the means of removing, by hallucinatory satisfaction, mental stimuli that disturb sleep.... Every time that we fully understand a dream it proves to be a wish-fulfilment, and this coincidence cannot be accidental or unimportant."[3] Hatterr has many dreams which show his subconscious fears and hopes and throw light upon his personality. For example, Hatterr enters into a dream-world after undergoing a traumatic experience in the circus when he had to act as a 'human plate' for the lion to eat the mutton-piece. The dream has three phases. In this dream one can easily see how dream symbolism and numerological symbolism are interwoven. In the first phase, Hatterr finds himself in North Dakota and sees the convocation of graduates there especially Ph.Ds and M.Ds. There are twelve graduates in all of which six are tall and six dwarf. One of the dwarf guys wants to deliver thirteen telegrams for two bucks each. But Hatterr has no money at all to buy one of the telegrams from Lord Nuffield. In spite of the apparent absurdity of the dream, one may interpret it as a wish-fulfilment of Hatterr's secret desire to be formally educated at a University, as his very presence among the graduates symbolises. The dream also symbolises his pauperism by showing his inability to buy the telegram with two rupees. The reason why the telegrams have to be bought by the parties cannot be ascertained as it may easily be ascribed to the absurd element in the dream. The numerological symbolism of six dwarfs and six graduates making a total of twelve may be interpreted in the following way : "Twelve (3×4; 5+7) is the great cosmic number."[4] It easily indicates some kind of order in the universe. In Sumer and China it is the number of signs of the zodiac and the basis of sexagesimal system. Similarly the twelve tribes of Israel, the twelve disciples of Christ and that twelve gates of heavenly Jerusalem are well-known examples in the history and literature of the world. If the twelve graduates of North-Dakota symbolise an order and balance, Hatterr being the thirteenth person indicates that he is an unwanted and unlucky fellow upsetting the order or evenness. Thirteen "Thirteen (12+1) disrupts the perfection of the duodecimal system and being connected with the inter-calary month, was considered unlucky in Babylon...."[5] Likewise number thirteen is associated with superstitions. As pointed out by Bertrand Russell, "Among ourselves the prejudice against...number 13 is very active, ...many hotels have no 13th floor."[6] Usually number 12 and 13 are found to be closely associated on many occasions. For example one leader with twelve followers, twelve jury headed by one judge and twelve open rooms and one closed room are commonly associated in world literature and life. In the present novel the twelve graduates and the thirteenth uneducated person *i.e.* Hatterr symbolise Hatterr's ill-luck and his oddness there in the atmosphere.

Further, the telegrams, according to our routine experience, are coded or cryptic messages from somebody. Hatterr's inability to buy one of those telegrams easily symbolises his badluck preventing him from knowing the secret or message sent to him by some unknown source or God thereby keeping him in perpetual insecurity of ignorance about life.

The second part of his dream shows Hatterr's entry into St. Paul's Church of London. According to Freudian interpretation "churches and chapels are symbols of a woman."[7] Hatterr's entry into the church may be Freudianly interpreted as symbolic of his latent desire for entry into a woman. One may also easily see in this dream the easy translatability of spirituality and sexuality into each other. His sight of 'an inconceivably beautiful coffin' being carried into the church and being fixed with a tin plate containing Hatterr's name and countless degrees and honorifics like Ex-Sahib, Ex-Sportsman, Ex-human, Ex-parte may be taken to symbolise his own metaphorical death or wish for death, perhaps caused by his forlornness and deep frustration in life. But the dream may also be taken to be symbolic of Hatterr's wishful glorification of himself even after his death in the form of being sealed in a beautiful coffin displaying his name with innumerable degrees on the tinplate. This part of the dream shows the contradictory element of his frustration and helplessness and metaphorical death on the one hand and the element of his desire for glorification even in death, on the other. The contradictory nature of his dream appears to be in tune with his own philosophy which declares that life is nothing but a bundle of contrarieties.

The third and last phase of his dream shows his admittance into the surgical ward in the hospital, for an operation on him for the removal of his appendix. The doctors and nurses are employing infrared irradiation on him. But Hatterr quarrels with the doctor urging him not to take away his appendix as he mistakes the medical term 'appendicitis' for the textual term 'appendix' and opines that the appendix is even more important than the autobiography. Hatterr's entry into the hospital is likely to symbolise his fear of operation (may be, even of castration) while his quarrel with the doctor is absurd, though it throws light upon his literary aesthetics.

Freudian symbolism has a significant share in the novel. For Angus, the Occidental teacher of Sheik Ell Arabi, teacher of H. Hatterr, the necktie happens to be a symbol of masculine or phallic power. As pointed out by Freud, "A *tie*, being an object which hangs down and is not worn by women is clearly a male symbol...."[8] Decked with the necktie, Angus could kiss a high class woman under the table and succeeded by way of wenching in marrying a very talented society woman called Maggie. For Sheikh, the necktie is a 'mystic symbol', or 'mystic material.' But this symbolism assumes a comic touch about it when the reader discovers that mysticism is nothing but etiquette. Anyway, one thing is quite clear that the necktie is a symbol of power either phallic or social. Hatterr, therefore, asks for Sage Sheik Ell Arabi's neckwear but the latter is exasperated beyond measure as he does not want to part with the secret of his own prosperity. The Sage, in his anger, asks Hatterr to go back to the abstract-minded Sage of Madras. One may easily interpret Hatterr's request for the necktie as his desire for some kind of power and prosperity in life. The necktie, therefore, assumes double dimension in its symbolism *i.e.* both Freudian and Marxian.

Hatterr, as confessed by himself, has the habit of inviting dreams, especially when he is in India. In one of his dreams, he sees the maestro Toseanini in Milan conducting the Philadelphia Symphony Orchestra. The audience come to attend the function. This part of the dream may be taken to symbolise his megalomaniac tendency to be associated with the great people like musicians as in the present case. In the next part of the dream, Hatterr is about to offer a cigar to his escort and even ready to light it for her. But before he could do the chivalrous act, he is shocked by the unexpected arrival of his wife Rialto there who asks him not to go to the Mysore State. Hatterr's act of offering cigar to his escort and his readiness even to light it may be interpreted as symbolic of his deep-seated chivalrous nature unfortunately frustrated by his wife. The cigar being a phallic symbol, his chivalry may be taken to be tantamount to his latent desire for illegal sexual union with the escort, frustrated by his wife.

Hatterr experiences another dream when he is sleeping in the mudhouse in the jungle along with his master Ananda Giri-Giri. The mudhouse is generally accepted to be a symbol of human body and the jungle, of the wilderness of his passion in general. The mudhouse in the midst of a jungle is an appropriate symbol for Hatterr being surrounded by wild feelings. In his dream in the mudhouse, he assumes the name of His Honneur the Sage of Bhoola Bhoola Sing alias Hamer Mario D Cunha, D.Litt and is frightened by the serpent Desjardines Fellows and is, therefore, awakened by the fear. The dream may be taken to symbolise not only his desire for Sagehood and the Freudian fear of sex, but the conflict between Spirit and Flesh in general. The dream easily suggests Hatterr's being torn between contradictory tendencies.

After having a number of contradictory and frustrating experiences with six saints, Hatterr goes to the seventh mentor who is known as 1008 Sriman Guruji. In Hindu spiritual tradition, the numbers like 108 and 1008 are supposed to be holy and suggest 9 when totalled up. 108 happens to be a holy number as it is made of 54+54 fundamental letters or alphabets (*bījākṣaras*) uttered in ascending and descending order respectively for transcendental meditation. Likewise 1008 happens to be a holy number which is generally used by many Hindu monks, especially of North-India as a prefix to their names (of holy order). In spite of his attachment for literature and beauty, Hatterr is advised by 1008 Sriman Guruji to become a *yati*. Accordingly Hatterr becomes a swami by assuming the new name of the holy order *i.e.* 504 Yati Rambeli. Since he is the disciple of the spiritual mentor, he cannot be equal to the latter in spiritual achievement. His number 504 clearly shows that he is half of his guru who is 1008. Even then he may be said to be qualitatively equal to his *guru* as his number 504 will be 9 when totalled up. Number 9 is suggestive of nine planets or *navagrahas* and their auspicious aspects. As pointed out by Mircea Eliade, "Nine, as three times three, is the number of completion.... Christianity speaks of nine orders of angels, and Dante thus saw Beatrice as the embodiment of nine."[9] The numerological symbolism of 9 is thus of universal importance and acceptance. This number obviously indicates that Hatterr has at last been able to achieve some kind of completion or perfection and the attendant tranquillity of mind which is only a consequence of the resolution of tensions or contrasts of life.

After undergoing an abundant and multifarious experience in life, Hatterr codifies it in the form of epigrammatical sentences which he calls his *Thesis Proper* having eighty (8×10=80) paragraphs. The number of paragraphs may again be interpreted according to numerological symbolism. Eight, according to numerology, happens to be a symbol of good or good fortune not only in Eastern but in Western religions also. As Mircea Eliade says, "Eight, the double four, is associated with good fortune. In Judaism the eighth day is singled out for circumcision. Christian tradition sees in the eighth day (the day after Sabbath) the resurrection of Christ; hence eight points to eternity."[10] According to Harold Baley, number 8 has "from ancient times been the emblem of regeneration."[11] Number 8, according to Swedonberg, "corresponds to purification."[12]

Number ten also symbolises many positive things not only in Eastern and Western religions, but also in science. "Ten, the number of human fingers, and thus a basis of the decimal system, is connected with completion. In the decade, multiplicity returns again to unity and the system is closed. The Pythogoreans regarded ten as the perfect number, since it is the sum of the first four integers (1+2+3+4) and is represented in the perfect triangle."[13] Hebrew and Buddhist scriptures speak of 'ten' principles and Aristotle recognises 'ten' categories of thought. In the light of these ideas, Hatterr's *Thesis Proper* in eighty paragraphs may be interpreted as a record not only of the findings of his spiritual experiments, but also of their codification and categorisation. It symbolises the distillation of the categorical essence from his rich and complicated existence. It symbolises the completion of his quest for Truth and grasp of the unity of life in the apparent contradictions and multiplicity of existence. It suggests the purification of his soul and its liberation from the dross of existence. It is indexical of his attainment of *Jīvan-mukta* stage or regeneration *i.e.* of being released from the bondage of this worldly life by transcending the contradictions of the phenomenal world.

In the sixteenth paragraph of his *Thesis Proper*, Hatterr mentions of his practice of wearing a magnetic waist-band of nine metals for health reasons. The nine metals are astrologically associated with the favourable effect of nine planets on the health of man. The practice indicates Hatterr's belief in the validity of astro-numerological symbolism.

In the twenty-ninth paragraph of his *Thesis Proper*, Hatterr confesses that he has tried to express the enigmatic quality of life in *seven* statements in his scenario. Numerologically speaking, seven can be symbolic of both holy and unholy aspects of life.

There is, thus, a preponderance of symbolism in the novel. Compared to symbolism, the allegorical element is very little. Hatterr, for example, has a tendency for allegorisation. In the fourteenth paragraph of his *Thesis Proper* he puts forth one of his formulae that living well is the best form of revenge and that the best physicians are Dr. Diet, Dr. Quiet and Surgeon Sir Bemerry. The medical truth has been personified in the form of these physicians who easily bring to our mind the allegorical characters found in the works of John Bunyan and Ben Jonson.

The symbolic element in the novel helps the novelist to express the initial tension in Hatterr's Eurasian sensibility followed by a resolution of tension and achievement of integration when he finally becomes a Hindu saint.

REFERENCES

1. Sigmund Freud, *A General Introduction to Psycho-Analysis.* Tr. by Joan Riviere (New York : Washington Square Press, 1968), p. 165.
2. Mircea Eliade, editor-in-chief, *The Encyclopaedia of Religion*, Vol. 11 (New York : Macmillan, 1987), p. 15.
3. Sigmund Freud, *A General Introduction to Psycho-Analysis*, p. 143.
4. Mircea Eliade, *The Encyclopaedia of Religion*, p. 17.
5. *Ibid.*, p. 17.
6. Bertrand Russell, *Unpopular Essays,* (Madras : Blackie & Son, 1977), p. 94.
7. Sigmund Freud, *A General Introduction to Psycho-Analysis*, p. 163.
8. *Ibid.*, p. 165.
9. Mircea Eliade, *The Enclopaedia of Religion*, p. 16.
10. *Ibid.*, p. 16.
11. Harold Baley, *The Lost Language of Symbolism*, Vol. II (London : Williams & Norgate, 1952), p. 45.
12. Quoted by Harold Baley, p. 45.
13. Mircea Eliade, *The Encyclopaedia of Religion*, p. 17.

[All the references to the text are from G.V. Desani's *All About H. Hatterr* (Harmondsworth : Penguin, 1972)].

2

Identity Crisis in the Novels of M.R. Anand

—Binod Mishra

> "Man's fate, today, is no longer in the hands of the gods, but is often in conflict with the evil in other men. Man makes himself, or thinks he can. The heart and mind of contemporary man is, therefore, moved by other casualties than salvation."[1]
>
> *—M.R. Anand*

MULK RAJ Anand, one of the triumvirates of the established Indian writers during the alien rule on our native land draws in characters from our everyday experiences presents them as they are. Not many authors before him could realize the importance of these non-entities and sympathize with their private tears and cheers. The unjust social and political order debases the qualities of human heart in his early novels. But this is only a fragment in his fiction. His hero in each novel shows courage and resilience and emerges from darkness and disruption.

The present paper aims to seek the crisis of identity Anand's characters suffer from. The pangs and suffering of his fictional figures bear the stamps of Anand who suffered the tedium of an empty and banal life where growth and self-awareness were thwarted. He writes with anguish that he grew up in a small world, materially poor and spiritually limited. His mother's influence 'permeated the very core of his being whereas his father's subservience gave him unmitigated despair. His university days were not happy. The murder of Yashmin, his beloved with whom he wanted to elope with deepened his despair. Foreign rule pricked his conscience. He was jailed for his campaign in 1921. He disgraced his family and his father fretted. Anand decided to go to England to escape from despair.

Anand tries to seek the causes of identity crisis in his characters. He's very close to Shelley who recognized man existing both as a social being and an imaginative individual. 'To exist' meant for Shelley a life lived in two worlds, the outer and the inner. Anand, like Shelley believes that every individual is an imaginative being and it's his imaginative mind that always seeks its identity with the universal system of things.

Anand's literary pilgrimage began with *Untouchable* (1935). The novel describes a day in the life of Bakha, a scavenger a well-built child of nature. His beautiful physical features have few takers. He becomes a victim of the prevailing caste-system during pre-independent India. The entire novel is the description of only one day when Bakha is slapped and for the only reason that he belonged to a low caste. The colony in which Bakha lives is dark and deep. When Bakha is slapped, he faces a crisis of identity. Critics may find the novel to be an attack on the caste-system but then it's also an individual's struggle against a sea of dogmas. Anand allows Bakha to confront with a reality that's stripped of all romantic illusions. The crisis of identity that Bakha faces characterizes and colours the personality of Bakha by his unquenchable wonder at life.

Bakha is a child of darkness, no doubt, but he derives his strength from the sun. His enormous capacity for work makes each muscle of his body shine forth like glass. He has his desires and dreams too. He, like every individual, longs for his identity. Anand describes the violent stirring in the soul of Bakha very candidly :

> "The accumulated strength of his giant body glistened in him with the desire for revenge while horror, rage, indignation swept over his frame."[2]

Dr. C.D. Narasimhaiah discovers in each novel of Anand "human centrality." He firmly affirms that *Untouchable* is not a propaganda piece because Bakha fights to seek his identity and steadfastness.

Bakha's bones are stiff and his flesh numb. But it does not numb his private feeling. His burning flames give him a sense of power. There are sores in his soul and his sense of segregation is corrosive. One can hear Bakha's self-cry in the following lines :

> "But the crowd which passed round him, staring, pulling, grimacing, jeering and leering was without a shadow of pity for his remorse."[3]

D. Reimenschender explores the problem of labour and fulfilment from a different angle. Since most of the Anand's heroes labour, it is viewed as an instrument of self-realization. If man is alienated from the product of labour it's a moment of despair. Reimenschender remarks :

> "If man is alienated from his own nature, he is also alienated from the human nature of his fellow beings a fact most obvious in the existence of antagonistic classes within a society."[4]

Perhaps the sugary tea which Bakha drank every morning, provided him with some fond experiences. More than the sweet tea and the sweet memory of his mother was his work, which gave him some triumph. Bakha's fight for his identity and survival get some consolation when the sister of Ramcharan creates for Bakha a new world full of wonder and enchantment. Bakha's feelings for that girl have been very graphically described in the novel :

> "There was something wistful about her, a soft light in her eyes for which she had become endeared to him. She had grown up to be a tall girl with a face as brown as ripe wheat and hair as black as the rain clouds."[5]

Bakha is trapped and is a victim of a recalcitrant society and he needs neither Gandhi nor Christianity but the poet who gives him a new vision to liberate him from his sickening surroundings.

The other two novels of the first trilogy, *Coolie and Two*

Leaves also run on the theme of exploitation and raise the question of identity crisis of their protagonists. Munnoo, the protagonist of coolie moves from the village to the town, from the town to the city and then to the mountains broadening the canvas of the novel. More extensive in time and space than the first novel, *Coolie* has an edge over *Untouchable*. Munnoo's experiences in Bombay and Daulatpur emphasize his savage struggle for survival. He endures the foul smell and stink, damp and sticky sweat, dust and heat and dung. Munnoo is a fragile boy in a hostile world. Life for him is a test of his vitality and impetuosity and his fundamental right to happiness is denied to him in a hostile climate. The cotton mills in Bombay where the boy has to work exposes him to the full force of the callous capitalistic order. He drifts into a more complicated and devious world. Munnoo represents the labour class and suffers the infernal miseries of the helpless labourers who are morbidly fatalistic. His cry for his identity is silenced by the deafening roar of the machine. It is not without irony that Munnoo is not willing to tear himself away from the sandy margins where he ran to the tune of lavish beauty. It is also not without irony that he traces the outlines of Sheela's figure with a delicate light on her regular mobile features. Munnoo's impetuosity, the utter humanness of his impulses, the sheer wantonness of his unconscious life force reveal his natural vitality. Munnoo dies and his death is a memorable and moving moment.

> "Munnoo clutches at Mohan's hand, felt the warm blood in his veins like a tide reaching out to distance to which it had never gone before."[6]

The opening line of the novel *Two Leaves and a Bud* — "Life is a journey into the 'unknown' hints at the crisis that it's packed with. The hero of the novel Gangu, an old and beaten man becomes a victim of colonial exploitation. The tragedy of the novel is unfolded against the dark backdrop of the tea plantation, which symbolizes the might and in-humanity of the British Empire. The coolies live in stifling surroundings and are part of the larger colonial experience. Gangu becomes a victim of man, god and civilization. He faces the storm, which ruins his harvest and shakes his identity. His wife dies in the lack of medical facilities and his world is broken. Even Gangu himself is killed while trying to save his daughter Leila from being defiled. His entire life is a saga of struggle and every moment he tries to safeguard his identity but fails. Much more than a scapegoat he sacrifices himself at the altar of the narrow racial prejudice. But he is not without zeal and zest for life. Anand writes :

> "He gripped the handle of his spade with an wavering faith and dug his foot into the sod made by a furrow and sensed the warm freshness of the earth that would yield fruit."[7]

Anand allows his characters to be more experienced in the second trilogy called Lalu-trilogy. The crisis of identity in this trilogy gains momentum and the claim for recognition becomes more extensive and existential. Where Bakha's crisis is born out of personal cry Lalu's is for broad identity. He becomes more of a patriot than a personal being and advocates for the release of his motherland from the clutches of an alien rule. The author in Anand who allowed his character in the first trilogy an arrest of energy, makes them struggle for release which will pave the path to freedom and joy. We find his characters maturing and educating themselves in the process of struggle and self-discovery. Anand, who gives voice to the voiceless, is of the belief that years of depression and dejection have strengthened their bones and a revolution seems at hand. He instills a hope in them as they grow to a full stature; he makes them realize that the ceremony of innocence won't always be drowned.

The Village (1939), *Across The Black Waters* (1941), *The Sword and The Sickle* (1942) deal with Lalu's despair. He is a young rebel bubbling with energy and vibrating with dreams and determined to reject all the prohibitions and prescription of the conservative Indian society. His haircut is considered as the worst kind of transgression. His crushed identity forces him to run away from his society and join the war as a professional soldier in the second novel. But his dreams are frustrated and his experiences strengthen his desire for introspection and exploration. The third novel, *The Sword and the Sickle* (1942) concludes Lalu's quest for self-actualization and self-realization on a note that is not rigidly ideological. When Lalu comes back to his country, he find its furrowed face unrecognizable. Lalu reconciles himself to his fate. He's imprisoned for his rebellion and from the jail he gives his countrymen the message of love, non-violence and togetherness. His despair is the result of the constant awareness of a split in his consciousness. He is shocked to realize that he is also a victim of the age-old inheritance. Lalu faces the fury of his father and his hair cut is viewed as the most terrible insult to his religion.

The basic question that gives a sharp focus to the whole gamut of Lalu's experiences is the question about his identity and destiny, which cannot be separated from his despair and delight. Lalu is in a constant state of tension because he is determined to rebel against the unthinking, unfeeling hierarchy perpetuated by vested interests in India. He is different from the ostracized Bakha or the pensive Munnoo or the aged and ineffectual Gangu. If Anand underrates the conscious factor and presents the revolutionary hero in a sketchy manner, he is not willing to succumb to the facile victory that characterizes the Marxist literature. What is more important for Anand is the question of survival, which absorbs all the energy of his hero. The second trilogy is more epical containing the whole gamut of human experience with the dynamic hero at the centre. Moreover, the trilogy emphasizes forcefully the reassertion of faith in the struggle to live, to grow and to fight for survival. Lalu is able to re-organize his personality and the important part of his mission is that the individual has to be saved. Lalu tempers his youthful recalcitrance and the constant process of introspection has its share of despair and delight. R. Shepherd very perceptively remarks :

> "Lalu's dilemma is one of conflicting loyalties. He is torn between past errors, the present commitments and the future aspiration."[8]

Lalu's attitude to Gandhi shows his despair because he does not share the superhuman qualities prescribed by Gandhi for the salvation of mankind. All the lofty notions of Gandhi like suffering; soul-force self-perfection and sublimation are alien to the exuberant and turbulent self of Lalu. Terrorism is as disgusting to Lalu as self-righteousness. What gives Lalu real joy is love and understanding which is more important and more effective than any political or religious dogmas. He knows that only Maya could give him the pulsing warmth in a world vitiated by caution, fear and resentment. We find in the given lines how the private and the public concerns create a tension in his character :

> "Perhaps he felt there was nothing concrete in the outside world to cling to. He had never really becomes master of himself, of his destiny and was susceptible to all the weaknesses in his nature."[9]

The Big Heart (1945), *The Road* (1963) and *The Death of a Hero* are also dominated by the young protagonists who symbolize the spirit of joy. Though the characters in these novels also undergo sickness, morbidity and enertia but every moment of their life is strewn with despair. Anant in *The Big Heart* lives in a village which is a confusing jumble of the old and the new beliefs. He symbolizes the new upsurge in opposition to the old orthodoxy. The identity crisis in this novel gains a wider scope and Anant's revolutionary ideas are for the welfare of the whole and not of his own alone. Anant becomes the victim of Ralia's untamable fury and is killed. Ralia's vindictive passion and malice are the result of his ignorance. Anant symbolizes each impulse of life and tries to master his destiny by battling with the despair and abolishing unnecessary suffering. There are cankers in his soul but he keeps a vigilant eye on them. He was determined to 'outflank' his destiny and his commitment to truth was absolute. His commitment was not only to himself but also to those who, like him suffered the crisis of identity. We can note the sores in his soul :

> "No God, he felt could make such a world and consign it to such suffering for if he did so, he was not a good God."[10]

The crisis of identity acquires cosmic proportion in this novel. What Anant symbolizes in human and spiritual terms is more important than the way he is destroyed. Anant's trust in the here and now, his faith and pity and compassion and recognition of the dignity of man delights the reader. The irrational desires of the people — the fears, the prejudices and the suspicion are the real threats to the joy of the individual. Anand laments that the individual is in a mouse-trap. He allows the protagonist to express his crisis :

> "Caught in the mouse-traps where they are born, most of them are encaged in the bigger cage of fate and the various indiscernable shadows that hang over their heads."[11]

Bhikhoo in *The Road* is a victim of casteism. More organized and articulate than Bakha, Bhikhoo too faces the crisis of identity. But he symbolizes a climate of new togetherness. It's a moment of joy and consolation to him that Rukmini, the landlord's daughter responds to his love even in the face of hostility from her society. She rages against her father and brother who bring the disaster to the untouchables. Bhikhoo's crisis gets some moment of relief in the silent steady gaze of Rukmini.

Death of a Hero (1964), dealing with the disruption and disorientation and the communal frenzy, shows its protagonist's idea of death because he knows that the blind orthodoxy will frustrate all his positive and humanistic ideas and idealism. The novel shows Maqbool's consciousness of his identity. He is self-willed and not "wrapped up in the symbols of religious negation." The agonizing awareness of fear and hostility makes him passive and pensive. Maqbool fights the monsters and dies a glorious death. He symbolizes a new myth without which national resurgence cannot have any meaning. As a poet it is his mission to fire the imagination of the whole nation. His suffering is coloured with a longing of the welfare of humanity. He tells his sister :

> "It is a question of faith, of belief in ourselves and in the struggle. And then we can hope to be free. We shall have to suffer and suffer but that is how man grows."[12]

Maqbool's letter found from his pocket after his death records his dreams of the nation and the heroic deeds of the people. All this for him constitutes the heritage of struggle. Dr. Balram Gupta describes Maqbool's death as the harbinger of real triumph. Maqbool can be viewed as a positive image because he has the radiance of an unrepressed joy in contrast to the inward darkness of Bakha, Munnoo and Gangu. He emphasizes the urge for freedom from the heritage of struggle and the love of life.

We find echoes of identity crisis in the novel *Private Life of an Indian Prince* (1953) but in different way. The hero of the novel Vicky brings crisis in his life because of his own infirmities. His despair is rooted in the various strains that remain unrecognized in his personality. He is a pathetic captive of the chaning colours of enchantress Gangi's moods. The colours of her lust and passion give the prince unending thrill and excitement. The enchantress puts a new zest into the banal life of the prince. What brings crisis for the prince is his enormously enlarged ego, which remains unappeased in the newly emerging democratic climate of the country. The inner and outer disruption, the cancer of doubt, and the lack of stable temperament paralyze the prince. It's the thwarted love of the prince for the hill woman that gives him pangs and despair. It is not without irony that his emotion for the woman does not grow into a bright creative aura. The pull of carnal desire may be normal but what is abnormal is the ugly fact that Gangi is "coiled up in the entails of the prince." The story of the prince illustrates that we have a large heritage of darkness in the subterranean caves of our nature. What gives despair to Anand is the lack of will and the lack of creative purpose in life. The madness of the prince may be a complex event but it is not positive. The prince is destroyed by the dark seething waves that well up from the within. Vicky's suffering according to Dr. K.N. Sinha, is without delight because it is not transformed into 'spiritual torment.' The prince brings for himself only despair because his madness is not lit up by "the glimmer of self-knowledge." Apart from Vicky's personal despair the novel is a study of man's dreams and desires as stated forcefully by Dr. Shankar, his friend physician :

> "I believe in men. They have a great vitality, in spite of humiliation they have suffered. I do not believe that there is a soul distinct from the body. The soul is the body and the body is the soul and together they make a man. Mysticism is the approach of a dying man. Man is the final fact of the universe. There is nothing higher than human existence. I do not believe there is any power transcending man who decides things for him."[13]

Anand lived in an age that threatened the individual's sense of personal meaning. He wrote autobiographical novels to secure that sense of self. The problem of identity was for Herbert Read, 'an effective death protest against the permeating power of collective death-wish.' His autobiographical novel breaks the vice of reticence and overwhelms the readers with the expressive emotional honesty in all the four volumes — *Seven Summers* (1951), *Morning Face* (1968), *Confessions of a Lover* (1976) and *The Bubble* (1984). His confessions in these novels are secularized rather than sacramental. Individuation and not salvation is his central pre-occupation in these novels. Everything is subordinated to the act of self-exploration and self-actualization. Anand raises a cluster of awkward questions about authentic living, which divorces itself neither from pain nor from pleasure.

Anand is at his best in expressing the identity crisis in his autobiographical novels. It is in them that he puts joys and sorrows of his heart. His earlier novels may have their epical range but their framework hindered the novelist from unlocking the secret of his heart. His autobiographical novels enable the collective consciousness of India. Anand confesses candidly :

> "The connection between my life and writing is more intimate than in other novelists. I write as I live. My life is my message."[14]

Anand choose Krishan as the protagonist of his autobiographical novels. Krishan's acquaintance with the world, which offers him attraction and distractions and also challenges gradually deepens his vision of life. The rose buds and the scratches of the thorns were the sweet and bitter experiences of the growing child. Death as a dark reality hovers menacingly in the opening pages of the novel *Seven Summers* (1951). The outbursts of Krishan's feelings have the ample proof of an individual's crisis :

> "I closed the eyes against Prithvi's face that seemed to be coming towards me from a far land he had gone nearer and nearer, for I was sure that he would return. Darkness descended on me. Sleep. There was nothing more."[15]

Krishan lives in a precarious, fragile world full of silences. Turbulence and silence are the two poles showing his identity. The child always symbolizes terrific high spirits. The earth and the sky grew bigger and bigger for him during those days. His eyes were consumed by the dreads and fantasies. Even the dissolute fields overgrown with cactus and stubble fascinated him. Krishan is a growing child responding to the changing situations of life with uncommon courage and candour. He dismisses disdainfully his father as a patched-up compromise of the mechanistic Europe and feudalist Asia. The father could not analyze the feelings of his son because the struggle for existence had ruined his sensitivity. Krishan hated his mother in her sacred mood of worship because she looked distant and detached.

Anand dispenses with the third person narrative method in his autobiographical novels and adopts confessional method to capture the colour and texture of the protagonist's emotions and thoughts. There is a definite process of development in his fiction. The growth of self-awareness takes a more definite shape in *Morning Face* (1968). The protagonist enacts the drama of existence in its love-hate relationship in the phenomenal world.

The panoramic background of struggling India adds to the pattern of identity crisis a new dimension. The focus in the novel is, however, fixed on the protagonist and his evolution to higher consciousness. The clash of faiths in the home of protagonist shakes his identity. He does not respect the sane suggestions of his father, breaks the curfew and is punished for that. The merciless massacre at Jallianwallah Bagh completely alienates him from father. Anand describes his anguish in the following lines :

> "I now began to realize acutely the nature of difference between the two worlds in which I lived, the world of the compromise of my father and the world of the principles of the nationalist."[16]

This is symbolic of the clash between tradition and change. Krishan looks for an outlet for expressing the energy of volcano latent in his being. His aggressive egoism expresses itself in his campaign against the elders, against the supreme God and against his father.

The death of Kaushalya is the first crack in the consciousness of the adolescent protagonist. The marriage of his elder brother is for him is an institutionalized suppression. Krishan's despair is deepened by women in this novel. Devaki, Mumtaz and Shakuntala nourish the protagonist emotionally. Krishan loved Shakuntala for her courage and candour in a climate of sycophancy and hypocrisy. She gave sustenance to his emotional life. Krishan's quest for love gradually transforms itself into his quest for truth. His struggle for achieving a new identity continues in his confession of a lover with greater force and unrelenting tenacity. He is determined to resurrect his self. He has to distill all his experiences into a metaphysical pattern. What Iqbal says in his *Secret of the Self* stirs up the consciousness of Krishan in a profound way. Anand takes Iqbal's admonition with all sincerity and seriousness :

> "Read, read everything that comes your way. You can grow, everyone can. Only life and more life. Taste it and see it. It is bitter sweet."[17]

Self-awareness is, for Krishan, not an escape but a way of grappling with the world. It is his experience of love, its despair and delight that widen his consciousness. The love between a Hindu boy and a married Muslim woman has various ramifications. When Krishan loves Yashmin, he finds in her all the beauty and moisture of the earth and water.

Anand shows his exuberance and zest for life fully in his internationally acclaimed novel *The Bubble* (1984) wherein Krishan's consciousness is wafted into new areas. Krishan's identity as an Indian, who is not prepared to annihilate his root, is shaken. His encounters with a number of situations and personalities give him the best kind of education in England. What gave him dread and despair is the split existence in England. He is determined to gather the new sensations in England for his self-discovery. Krishan shows his full faith in Iqbal's mysticism when he says :

> "So to exist is to be. And to be is to become aware. Matter cannot become. Every new experience makes me. I can choose to be. Nature cannot. I have the freedom of choice. I can create myself through my consciousness."[18]

Anand records in his masterpiece *The Bubble* various events and situations, which help his characters, undergo the process of self-discovery. The self in contemporary society is fragmentary. Krishan tries to find his hidden selves through expiation and re-examination. He is able to achieve some kind of a structured whole. His ability to find larger frames of meaning gives his sense of significance as an individual. He does not lose his grip on life because he does not lack the structure of meaning. He does experience boredom and depression, but they do not weaken his will to live. Man is a teleological animal and his pure survival does satisfy his need for significance. Krishan is full of despair when Prof. Dicks dismisses India as a mumbo-jumbo. He remembers gratefully the phrases of Dayal Singh to counter the feeling of Prof. Dicks :

> "Man is on a journey to the unknown sun. But he has no shelter. He seems uprooted. He has to find a home in ecstasy."[19]

Krishan does not appreciate Gautam's stress on the effacement of the self and his Nirwana is, for Krishan, the state of nothingness. Love, hate, adversity and death are the facts of existence and they have much to do with the evolutionary process of life. Krishan writes in his letter to his friend, Noor :

> "The wish to move forward filled me with a warmth, that urged me on. I wanted to live, to breathe, to expand my soul, to run wild."[20]

Krishan's encounter with women paves the path to his progress. Women bring a transformation in his character. Evelyn reveals the platonic aspect of love, whereas Lucy symbolizes innocence and purity. She is part of negation and emptiness symbolized by Buddha whose philosophy is for Anand bereft of drama and magic. It's Irene who like Clara gives Krishan the desired ecstasy and fulfilment. Irene liberates him from all the fear and terror into an ocean of light. He feels lighter when there is a physical union between the two. Yashmin had given his some warm glimmering and her frail body gives him despair while the changing hues and the varying moods of Irene's face give him the joy of self-discovery. Life, for Krishan, is not only the rhythmic flow of nerves but also the renewal of vibrations within. Anand may be criticized for emphasizing much on body in *The Bubble*. But he doesn't like to call body a prison house and an isolated lump of flesh and bone. The body is a living link with the world and it is more a liberator than a fetter. If love is an outflow of surplus energy it has something to do with the self of the vital needs of the body. Krishan shows that a life of ideal harmony is not possible without an awareness of the body. It is body, which gives him the sense of his identity and harmony with the universe. This creates in him the feeling of wholeness.

Anand's women characters, too, share the equal identity crisis. They are soft, sober, suppressed and subjected to persecution yet they are sublime. It's in *The Old Woman or The Cow* that we find Gouri struggling against all odds to secure her identity. Her silent suffering climaxes into the delightful moment of her complete liberation. She slams the door against her husband and explodes the old myth of the suffering and enduring Sita devoured by the earth. Gouri's life is a pilgrimage of hope and faith. Her inner transformation is a moment of triumph that gives no delight. She is not like Noor who succumbs to despair. She organizes her emotions to bring substance and significance. She doesn't allow her cultural conditioning to deform her into an image of self-surrender and despair. Likewise, Gangu's daughter, Leila in *Two Leaves* radiates with a new light. Anand shows his greater admiration for women in general and Gangu's wife in particular when he says :

> "There is something of water about a woman. Flowing, always flowing one way or another; restless like the waves, sometimes overwhelmingly moody fickle and capricious as a river in a storm, sometimes bright and smiling, sometimes soft and sad but always tender and king."[21]

Thus we find that the individual's search for identity is the central preoccupation of Anand in most of his novels. To A.V. Krishna Rao, this is a stage of synthesis in which the private and the public components of life are integrated. The loss of identity in his novels is a moment of despair for the hero but when he regains his identity after a prolonged struggle, it is a moment of delight for him. The fact that Anand's hero is not without grit and guts gives the readers delight. The quest theme which is found in every novel has its share of despair and delight. Anand's hero in each novel grows and becomes progressively more sure of himself passing from a low level of consciousness to a more happy adulthood. The turbulent moment born out of his encounter with other points of view is a creative crisis full of despair and delight. The critical juncture in each novel tests resources and resilience of the hero. The fact that the opposing images of the individual and society are fused, emphasizes the primacy of delight. The evolution of a new self for each hero through strain and tension towards hope and fulfilment is a familiar pattern.

Anand believes that man can emerge from the breakdown, the disruption and the decay. Poverty and hunger inspire courage. Man can contend with the disruptive forces and can conquer them. If there's discord in life it is a stage and not a terminus. Life is a pattern of despair and delight and it is not without its dynamic thrust. Man has to make and re-make himself for an authentic living. The nightmare of living in a hostile world brings fear and disquiet for men but the solitary contemplative sinks again into the quiet of self-communion. Man has in him not only the noises of the earth but also the silence of the seas and music of the year. Anand's characters suffer the crisis of identity no doubt, but on regaining their identity after a prolonged struggle it's a moment of delight for them. Radhakrishnan, too, endorses what the protagonist of Anand's novel does;

> "For the flower to develop the bud has to die, for the fruit the flower, for the seed the plant and for the plant the seed. Life is a process of eternal birth and death. All progress is sacrifice."[22]

NOTES & REFERENCES

1. M.R. Anand, "The Story of My Experiments with a white lie," in *Critical Essays* ed. M.K. Naik, p. 16.
2. M.R. Anand, *Untouchable*, p. 57.
3. *Ibid.,* p. 55.
4. Dieter Reimenschneider, "Alienation in the novels of Anand", in *Perspective*, ed. by K.K. Sharma, p. 96.
5. M.R. Anand, *Untouchable*, p. 97.
6. M.R. Anand, *Coolie,* p. 318.
7. M.R. Anand, *Two Leaves and a Bud*, p. 146.
8. R. Shepherd, "Alienated Being" in *Perspectives,* p. 143.
9. M.R. Anand, *The Village*, p. 229.
10. M.R. Anand, *The Big Heart*, p. 68.
11. *Ibid.*, p. 17.
12. M.R. Anand, *Death of a Hero.*
13. M.R. Anand, *The Private Life.*
14. P.K. Rajan, *Studies in M.R. Anand*, p. 95.
15. M.R. Anand, *Seven Summers*, p. 23.
16. M.R. Anand, *Morning Face*, p. 438.

17. M.R. Anand, *Confession of a Lover,* p. 160.
18. M.R. Anand, *The Bubble*, p. 72.
19. *Ibid.*, p. 18.
20. *Ibid.*, p. 81.
21. M.R. Anand, *Two Leaves*, p. 148.
22. M.R. Anand, *Preface to Apology for Heroism,* p. 99.

3

Ontological Entity in Raja Rao's *The Serpent and the Rope*

—Ramesh Kumar Gupta

RAJA RAO is a very distinguished name in the fictional world today, and his novels and short stories have attracted much critical perception. The ontological aspect of his fiction has chiefly intrigued a number of critics in India and abroad. The novelist's urge to know the reality reveals that he has an ontological psyche. His announcement that "I have abandoned literature for good and gone over to metaphysics"[1] indicates that Raja Rao's panoramic view is expressively ontological. He tries to be metaphysician in outlook and experience when he observes that he sees "but metaphysical proposition everywhere."[2] He concedes that "one can realize one's metaphysical entity by a keen perception of primordial Indian reality."[3] He has entrusted to one of his interviewers in India that it "has been my endeavour all my life to be face to face with the ultimate."[4]

Raja Rao's second novel *The Serpent and the Rope* (1960) is profoundly rooted in Indian Ontology, it portrays man's quest for self-realization. The ontological motto of this novel is "waves are nothing but water. So is the sea."[5] The theme of this novel, as Rao observes, is "the futility and barrenness of man in human existence when man (or woman) has no deep quest, and no thirst for the ultimate. Man's life here in Samsara is an august mission to find the Absolute."[6] This theme is elucidated in the very first sentence of the novel through the narrator-protagonist, K.R. Ramaswamy, who desires to know the Reality. Born a Brahmin, he seeks Brahman. He holds that "Brain is he who knows Brahman."[7] It is considered the mouthpiece of the novelist. In this interview with Shiva Niranjan, Raja Rao also admits that "Ramaswamy is myself."[8] Ramaswamy knows that existence is a voyage between birth and death.

The Seprent and the Rope is impregnated with philosophy generally construed to be Vedantic. To attain self-realization, Ramaswamy wishes to follow the non-dualistic philosophy of Sankara. Referring to this novel, M.K. Naik remarks : "This Advaitic doctrine of the identity of Jiva and Siva forms, as seen earlier, the very basis of the novel."[9] C.D. Narasimhaiah observes Ramaswamy-Savithri relationship covered with an effect of Vedantic spirituality as he likens the lovers with Siva and Parvati — "the Absolute in union with the Absolute to be one."[10] Narasimhaiah highlights the salutary love of Savithri for Ramaswamy. He blinks a significant notion of their love which is extrawedding — a kind of love deliberated typically in Tantrism in that it is free from social and moral obligations. S.C. Harrex points out the performances of Rao's characters in this novel in terms of ontological entity. E.J. Kalinnikova affirms that Raja Rao is a Vedantist and he discusses the Advaita Vedanta of Sankara in his works. In *The Serpent and the Rope* Kalinnikova experiences the primus symbol of the rope which is usually taken for the serpent serves as a "superb poetical example to prove the illusory nature of the world and this kind of vision is unmistakably Vedantic."[11] The analogy of the serpent and the rope is, no doubt, derived from the non-dualistic philosophy of Sankara. Sankara says in *Vivekachudamani* : "The rope is supposed to be the snake only so long as the mistake lasts, and there is no more snake when the illusion has vanished. Similar is the case here."[12] It is only because of ignorance that the rope appears to be snake. The world, being the effect of nescience, is only an appearance, and not a reality. In *The Serpent and the Rope*, Ramaswamy says, the "world is either unreal or real — the serpent or the rope. This is no in-between-the-two and all that's in-between is poetry, is sainthood" (p. 335).

Ramaswamy's statement that the "world is either unreal or real" is different from the world of Sankara. He says that the world of experience is full of repugnances and an object of knowledge cannot be stated as real. The world is not present at all times, so it is not real. The world which has its beginning and is incessantly changing cannot be real. Sankara explains : "What is eternal cannot have a beginning and whatever has a beginning is not eternal."[13] On this wise, the world is neither real nor unreal. The world which is not real has its foundation in Brahman. Brahman is the underlying basis of the world as the rope is the basis of the serpent. Ramaswamy's perception that we run and lament as we see a serpent (p. 335) corroborates Sanakara's observation that a "man may in the dark mistake a piece of rope for a snake and run away from it, frightened and trembling."[14] The dark is the emblem of nescience and the world is the result of Maya. Here Rao agrees with the statement made by Sankara that maya conceals the real (rope) and projects the unreal (snake).

In the ontological novel *The Serpent and the Rope* it is the re-discovery of India and the re-illustration of Indian religious philosophy. Ramaswamy, who relates the sad and uneven chronicle of a life with no art or adornment but with the objectivity, the order of the historical sciences, is especially suited for this role. In this novel, the philosopher novelist interprets, from the learned South Indian Brahmin's point of view, the Illusion and the Reality as a Vedantin looks at the world and at India in particular. Ramaswamy after his sojourn in France where he led a married life with a French girl, Medeleine, realises on his return to India that the whole European culture or the materialistic civilization is only an illusion like the Serpent, while the Indian spiritual Advaitic Vedanta based vision is the Reality, the Rope. In the ontological entity Ramaswamy conveys his awareness of spiritual experience :

> "In experience, there is no object present.
> There is only experience."
> "Well, how is that?"

> "The sensation must finish its function before knowledge dawns. In knowledge there is no object present — if so, who has knowledge of it? You might say, 'I'. And the I has the knowledge of the I through —?"
> "Through knowledge", said Madeleine.
> "So knowledge has knowledge of the I through Knowldege which means knowledge is the 'I'.
> "Yes, that it so." (p. 112)

To acquire the knowledge of Sivoham by experiencing the Self Ramaswamy begins a divine journey in the novel. He emphasizes the idea that in the spiritual experience, the subject and the object, the knower and the known are unified. Ramaswamy in this novel assigns similar characteristics to Brahman :

> "Not hearing nor tasting nor smelling or seeing,
> But Form of Consciousness and Bliss;
> Shiva I am, I am Shiva." (p. 114)

Ramaswamy's ideas on death have been derived from the *Upanisads*. He throws light on it and says nobody has died in that birth and death are the 'illusions of the non-self' (p. 16). Whenever a person dies, the soul (Atman) just changes its apparel. *Srimad Bhagwad Gita* asserts the immortality of the soul. The same idea is mentioned in *Katha Upanisad* too : "If the slayer thinks that he slays or if the slain thinks that he is slain, both of them do not understand."[15] Under the influence of these Vedantic perceptions, Ramaswamy understands that his son Pierre, his mother Gauri and his father are not truly dead because the 'soul' in them is immortal and imperishable. To Ramaswamy death does not exist. Emancipation in the Hindu tradition is emancipation from the cycle of reiterated births and deaths. He looks upon death as a mystery but nevertheless confides in the iteration of life. The ontological world is bound by the law of cause and effect. To obtain immortality, Ramaswamy emphasizes the myth of Satyavan and Savithri :

> "Will you exchange place with me?" I asked.
> "Yes, if you like this wretched cloak."

> "If you become me, then there is no problem."
> "How so?"
> "Then you, become me, will be the real Savithri."
> "And who's the Satyavan?"
> "The Self, the Truth," I said... "No, Satyavan cannot die."
> "Man must unto himself be himself and his bride. You remember
> I told you, all brides be Benares born." (p. 360)

Raja Rao's concept of "isness", "I" and "Truth" ingrained in this novel is the essence of ontological entity. The first definition of "isness" by Siddha Rahulbhadra is the state of ultimate bliss (*dharmamahasukha)*.[16] Raja Rao also elevates "isness" as Truth which he confides is synonymous with "I" or "bliss". In one of the ontological discussions in the novel, Ramaswamy and Savithri conclude that "isness" is the Truth :

> "Therefore, What is Truth?" I asked....
> "Isness is the Truth", she answered. (p. 130)

Saraha peceives that "the aspirant will attain the ultimate bliss of "isness" when his mind is completely and unshakably peaceful and he gets lost in bliss as salt in water."[17] By the dispersion of salt into water, the salt loses its identity and becomes water itself. Such maxim in the novel expressively points to the state of "isness" which may be reached by having recourse to the condition of "no-mind". Ramaswamy attests "isness" in his newly born son Pierre who is the haughty test of joy. Pierre is the emblem of blessing : "He was proof that man is, and cannot be happy but be happiness itself" (p. 38). His newly born babe Pierre is not conscious of his mind, he is in a state of "isness" or complete bliss. His mind is "no-mind", completely light and purely free and, therefore, happy.

Raja Rao points out the mystical aspect of woman. Sita in Rao's short story "Javni" says that man can never understand woman. This mystical awareness is also referred to in *The Serpent and the Rope*. Madeleine says to Ramaswamy that no man knows a woman (p. 164). Saroja's beauty is a mystery to Ramaswamy. He declares that the young girl growing into woman is a mystery unobserved (p. 49). Ramaswamy credits that woman is a mystery to man as all wisdom is employed to know her. However, he believes if we understand a woman, we can never be a pilgrim to knowledge. Such concepts about the woman are based upon ontological entity. *Yoginihrdaya Tantra* portrays that woman is baffling mystery : Only Siva knows the heart of woman.[18] The novelist insists on the non-dual identity between man and woman. Ramaswamy affirms that man is incomplete sans woman : "If there were nothing other, you could not know that you are" (p. 170). He again says that man "sees himself in woman as essence, the fact of womanhood is the meaning of his life" (p. 170). It reveals that identity-experience between man and woman. Herbert V. Guenther remarks that in order to "find himself man needs the 'other' who is no intellectual abstraction, but part of himself needed in order to be himself."[19] In the *Jnanamudra*, woman is regarded as a goddess and man realizes his "Being" (spiritual essence) through an identity-experience with her.[20] Savithri proves that Ramaswamy could be "I". The "I" here is not synonymous with the Cosmic Self but refers to man's "Being" which is experienced in the form of man and woman. Ramaswamy's assertion, "You can marry, when there is no one to marry another. The real marriage is like 00, not like 010" (p. 239), indicates that the real love is in sooth an identity-experience which assures perfect awareness, spontaneity and purity. H.V. Guenther states in *The Tantric View of Life* : "Here, in spontaneity which is non-dual and naturally pure, one's Being (belag-nyid), in order that one may understand One's Being, manifests itself in the shape of man and woman."[21] In *The Serpent and the Rope* Ramaswamy's encounter with Madeleine transports him into flights of perceptible rapture as he attempts to experience with Madeleine :

> "And Madeleine in there, with her hips so wonderous blue and red, and she smells, God, she smells of me, of my elephant, of my suchness, and I ask of her, and she murmurs such ontological things that her very eyes seem fixed; and taking me into myself, I transpire as the truth, as though touched by itself, like the wave that sees itself

> to be sea, like the earth that was spread out and was called Madeleine. But when I want to call her Madeleine, I have to say Rama — her lips are mine turned outward, her flesh mine turned inward.... And I take her away to a world from which there is no returning — like those Tibetan tanakas...and the music has been piping a long while...you accept gifts in between the acts, you touch the heart between the breasts; and you lie on Madeleine as though on a great sea-shore. The night has ended.... It's the time for ablutions, for the murmur of prayers and the road to the temple by the river. The God knows you and you know the God.... For a moment you had gone beyond the body (pp. 159-60).

Inspired by the ontological entity, Ramaswamy announces that man must incorporate the woman into himself. He insists on the interdependence of man and woman for the attainment of 'wholeness' : "The woman needs our worship for her fulfilment, for in worshipping her we know the world and annihilate it, absorbing it into ourself. We should be Shiva that woman be dissolved — and with her the world. For the world is meant not for denial but for dissolution" (p. 172). A woman requires man's adoration for her identity and satiation, the female ontologist may acquire the knowledge of androgyny by her absorption into man. Savithri, by this reason, ever discloses her desire for absorption : "To be a woman, she knew, was to be absorbed by a man" (p. 187).

Ramaswamy's reference to the harlots of Benares, who are extremely beautiful, has ontological entity in the novel. The punk's smile for a customer and their worship of the goddess Parvati for the safety of their beauty and youth suggest their yearning for eternity of love. It is well-known that the prostitutes of Benares are independent to love as they have risen above social and moral obstructions. He again refers to the love of *gopis* who loved Krishna beyond social inhibitions, in that their love for the god was real and eternal. This kind of free love has been frequently emphasized in the novel. Ramaswamy truly says : To be free is to know one is free, beyond the body and beyond the mind; to love is to know one is love; to be pure is to know one is purity. Impurity is in action and reaction : What is born must die, what has form must vanish and stink" (p. 382). The corporeal sins are no sins, for the body is mortal. That is why Rao believes that liberty or purity depends on man's own tendency.

Thus, Raja Rao depicts the ontological entity in *The Serpent and the Rope*. He is a mythmaker, a symbolist and a philosophically complex novelist. It may be noted that this novel is not only a metaphysical treatise but also a fictional work. Raja Rao's projection of ontological entity in his novel is best known as the aesthetic understanding of an imaginative writer who has given an distinctive form to Indian novel by correlating the Puranic mode of writing with western forms and ideas. As an imaginative writer, Raja Rao compares different philosophical points of view to describe the deep recesses of the human heart.

NOTES AND REFERENCES

1. Quoted in E.M. Forster : *A Tribute*, ed. K. Natwar Singh (Delhi, 1964), p. 17.
2. *Ibid.*, p. 28.
3. S.V.V., "Raja Rao : Face to Face", *The Illustrated Weekly of India*, 5 January, 1964, p. 45.
4. Shiva Niranjan, "An Interview with Raja Rao", *Indian Writing in English*, p. 20.
5. *The Serpent and the Rope* — Raja Rao — Dedication page.
6. Raja Rao's Letter to M.K. Naik quoted by Naik in his *Raja Rao*, p. 84.
7. Raja Rao, *The Serpent and the Rope.*
8. Shiva Niranjan, "An Interview with Raja Rao", *Indian Writing in English*, ed. Krishna Nandan Sinha (New Delhi, 1979), p. 25.
9. Quoted by M.K. Naik in his *Raja Rao* (1972); rpt. Bombay, 1982, p. 97.
10. C.D. Narasimhaiah, *Raja Rao* (New Delhi, n.d.), p. 12.
11. E.J. Kalinnikova, "Ancient Indian Philosophy and Raja Rao's Works", *Perspectives on Raja Rao*, ed., K.K. Sharma (Ghaziabad, 1980), p. 29.
12. Swami Madhavananda, trans., *Vivekachudamani of Sri Shankaracharya*, Seventh edition (1921; rpt. Calcutta, 1966), pp. 78-79.
13. Radhakrishnan, *Indian Philosophy*, II (1923, rpt. London, 1971), p. 563.
14. *Ibid.*, p. 580.

15. *Katha Upanisad*, 1.2.19.
16. Rahulbhadra quoted by S.K. Ramchandra Rao in *Tibetan Tantric Tradition* (New Delhi, 1977), p. 39.
17. Saraha quoted by S.K. Ramchandra Rao in *Tibetan Tantric Tradition*, p. 39.
18. Sir John Woodroffe, *Sakti and Sakta*, (Madras, 1975), p. 264.
19. Herbert V. Guenther, *The Tantric View of Life*, p. 67.
20. *Ibid*., p. 72.
21. *Ibid*., p. 67.

4

The Trauma of Partition in *Azadi*

—Basavaraj Naikar

CHAMAN NAHAL (1927 —) is hailed as a brilliant Indian English novelist of the second generation. He has enriched the field of political fiction which is very poor as compared to other forms of Indian English fiction. His *Gandhi Quartet* has an epic sweep covering the whole prospect of the Gandhian era in Indian life. *Azadi*, which happens to be one of the four novels of the *Gandhi Quartet* offers an intensive picture of the effect of the traumatic experience of the partition of the country into India and Pakistan on the life of the people living in the north-western border area of India. As all the historians and political thinkers of India know, the Indian freedom was won after a long struggle and sacrifice by the Indian leaders and masses. It remains memorable experience in the pages of Indian history. There are countless books and tracts dealing with the antecedents and consequences of partition, but the novels dealing with the same theme are very few in number. Khushwant Singh's *Train to Pakistan*, Malgonkar's *A Bend in the Ganges* are some of the very few Indian English novels depicting the deeply disturbing experience of partition. Chaman Nahal's *Azadi* belongs to this group of novels and succeeds in giving a very convincing and graphic picture of the horrors and paradoxes of partition experience felt by the people of north-western part of India around 1947.

Like a good creative writer, Chaman Nahal has depicted the horrors of partition experience by concentrating on the life of Lala Kanshi Ram of Sialkot, thereby highlighting the positive as well as the negative side of the complex problem. Lala Kanshi Ram, the protagonist of *Azadi* becomes a spokesman of the Hindus who are deeply disturbed by the unprecedented political event. Although the novel has been written from an omniscient point of view, it depicts life as seen through Lala Kanshi Ram's consciousness. Lala Kanshi Ram has been leading a contented life in Sialkot as a grain merchant. He has also bought a few acres of land in his native village. He has a pious and beautiful but illiterate wife, Prabha Rani whom he tries to educate perpetually. He has a daughter, Madhubala and a son, Arun. He has been living in a rented house belonging to Bibi Amarvati. He is a spirited Hindu who has great respect for Vedic philosophy. He knows Sanskrit, Hindi and Punjabi sufficiently well. A member of the Arya Samaj, he has great admiration for Hindu culture in general.

Since he has been living in a colonial situation, he has an ambivalent attitude towards the British Raj. Although as a Hindu patriot he hates the British people and their Government in general, he admires the discipline and precision of the British Raj. He, therefore, takes his son Arun to the Hurrah Parade and inspires him to watch the discipline of the British officers. The British soldiers' parade is disturbed by the stray dogs. The British sergeants, therefore, shoot the dogs deftly after the parade is over. Lala Kanshi Ram tries to see the principle of spiritual unity in human life and therefore thinks that even a Britishman is created by God. He believes that

> All created matter was one, man and beast and bird, and the flowers and the trees to boot. And these Angrez were another aspect of the same Brahman who constituted total reality.... Their Hurrah Parade had been ruined by these nasty dogs, which no one owned and which were a nuissance to the entire community. They must help them to corner these scavengers and destroy them... (p. 23).
>
> What mattered to Lala Kanshi Ram was the precision of the British Raj, which was seen in as small an act as the killing of a stray dog. No wonder they ruled the world

> over, no wonder, he said to himself. There indeed was no Raj like the Angrez Raj ! (p. 25)

There is, thus, a love-hate relationship between Indians and the British Government as symbolised by Lala Kanshi Ram's approach.

Lala Kanshi Ram observes with very keen interest the political turbulence that is going on in India during the pre-Independence years. Like all other Indians, especially Hindus, he hopes that India will achieve freedom sooner or later. He knows that Gandhi and Nehru and the other Congress leaders are trying their best to oust the British people from the country. But alas, their hope is not realised totally. Like Kanshi Ram, the members of his family and the neighbouring families listen to the radio regularly to learn the latest developments in the political arena. They fear about the creation of Pakistan which would create several problems for the country. He articulates his fear about the partition to his wife, "Everything will be ruined if Pakistan is created" (p. 34). Chaman Nahal offers a very subtle picture of Kanshi Ram's fear about the partition and the consequent problems that they will have to face :

> He saw his wife was frightened and he tried to stifle his anxiety. He had his fears since February, when the British set up a time limit for independence. They had clearly committed themselves; they had said that, not later than June 1948, India would have azadi. They also that if the Indian political parties did not agree on a solution by then, the British would hand power over to any constituted authority or authorities of the movement; but they must quit. It was this that disturbed Lala Kanshi Ram. Good, India would be free. But why were they in a hurry to leave? And why this reference to freedom in the plural? Didn't that mean they were thinking of Pakistan? And the Congress leaders — what trust could you put in them? Didn't Gandhiji and Rajaji themselves as much as offer Pakistan to Jinnah in 1944? They were the ones who put the idea in his head, if you ask me. Take a section in the East of India and a section in the West, they said. Only let's have a common defence and

> foreign policty. Until then Jinnah had talked of Pakistan, but did not quite know what he meant by it. Gandhi, by going to him, not only gave Pakistan a name, he gave Jinnah a name too. Who took Jinnah seriously before September 1944? It was doubtful if he took himself seriously, either. Ever since then he had been sharpening his teeth and becoming more and more menacing. If the Congress would give this much, why not go for complete separation? Gandhi had meanwhile asserted he would never accept *that*. Over our dead bodies alone, the Congress leaders said. We would shed the last drop of our blood, but we would not allow India to be partitioned. And now the English. Lala Kanshi Ram's last hope of peace on the sub-continent seemed to be giving in too (pp. 34-35).

Lala Kanshi Ram's premonition has finally come true. When he and the members of his family and those of the neighbouring families listen to the radio announcements, they are shocked out of their wits and feel deeply disconcerted. Lord Mountbatten, the Viceroy of India announces the Government decision on partition of the country into India and Pakistan :

> The Viceroy spoke in a clipped, sharp accent and even this non-English speaking audience could sense the emotion behind what he was saying. He was soon finished and all eyes turned first towards Suraj Prakash (since he was older of the two), who knew *some* English and when he threw up his hands in despair and shook his head.... Arun had understood it all only too well, and in a shaken voice he said, "Partition!' and made a gesture with his hands of chopping a thing in two. 'Partition!' many voices shouted out aloud and the mouths remained open. 'Yes, partition!' said Arun.
>
> Soon it was Pandit Nehru's voice coming through the radio and the audience was quiet again, though restless now, anxiously waiting for the English part of his speech to end so they could listen to him in Hindi. In both version Nehru spoke with much feeling, and with a sense of exhaustion rather than triumph. He had been acting as Prime Minister of the interim government since

> September 1946, and his voice had boomed on the air many times in the last nine months. Yet never before had he sounded so tired (pp. 57-58).

Once the inevitable partition is decided and announced, it creates a mental shock to the Hindus and the Sikhs who begin to worry about their future safety and peace. But the news creates a lot of jubilation among the Muslim population. Both the Hindus and Sikhs on the one hand and the Muslims on the other become suddenly aware of their separate identities. Whereas the non-Muslims feel insecure and fearful, the Muslims jubilate over partition by shouting slogans like 'Pakistan zindabad! Long live Pakistan!' etc., fire crackers, illuminate their houses with countless earthen lamps and take out processions in the main lanes of Sialkot. They display their joy by dancing, mock-fighting and singing and by forcibly taking the procession through the Hindu Mohulla where Lala Kanshi Rama and his friends live. The Police Superintendent and the Deputy Commissioner try their best to control the situation. The Hindus and the Muslims begin to hate and fear each other suddenly with some rare exceptions like Lala Kanshi Ram and Chaudhri Barkat Ali who had attended Gandhi's speech at Ramatalai in 1929. Both of them were deeply impressed by Gandhi's views on Hindu-Muslim unity, home industry, nationalism, Purna Swaraj, non-violence, self-discipline and self-sacrifice and had sworn to be life-long friends and never thought of the communal barrier between themselves :

> Immediately after the speech, and before, the reawed shouts of 'Mahatma Gandhi ki jai' had died down, Chaudhri Barkat Ali turned towards Lala Kanshi Ram and said seriously : 'You're my brother from today.'
>
> Lala Kanshi Ram chuckled. He had always regarded Chaudhri Barkat Ali as a brother, he did not need a Gandhi to make him aware of that (p. 101).

Whereas Chaudhri Barkat Ali represents sensible and humanistic Muslims, Abdul Ghani, the hookah-maker represents the irrational and fanatical Muslims. As soon as partition is declared by the government, he feels ecstatic about it and begins to hate and defy all the Hindus including Lala Kanshi Ram. He asks Lala Kanshi Ram as to when he is leaving Pakistan :

> "Why do you want me to leave, Abdul Ghani?" said Lala Kanshi Ram. 'We have been good friends — for years we have been such good friends!'
>
> Abdul Ghani was taken aback at this. He had other nasty things he wanted to say to Lala Kanshi Ram; he couldn't bring one of them out. Deflated, he sat on the wooden platform and looked at the ground.
>
> Remembering he was speaking to a kafir after all, he flared up again.
>
> 'I want you to leave because you're a Hindu, and you don't believe in Allah' (p. 128).

Thus even the good friends begin to drift apart because of the communal hatred aggravated by the partition of the country.

The communal hatred between the Hindus and the Muslims which was latent so far becomes blatant and expresses itself in so many details. The Muslims burn down countless houses of the Hindus, burgle their houses, rape the Hindu women and murder the Hindu population indiscriminately and ruthlessly. But unfortunately Hindus cannot retaliate strongly and properly because of lack of solidarity among themselves. There is a similar hatred between Muslims and Sikhs also. The Sikhs murder many Muslims. Some times they compromise with the situation by shaving their beard and removing the paraphernalia of Sikh symbols like turban and kangan etc. Thus there is a general atmosphere of mutual hatred, fear and distrust among the Muslims, the Hindus and the Sikhs. All of them suffer from some kind of psychological restlessness, anxiety and insecurity.

But the emotional relationship between man and woman is not at all affected by the communal hatred. Arun, son of Lala Kanshi Ram has been in love with Nur (Nisar Nurunnisa), sister of Munir. Both of them are students in the same (Murray) college. They meet secretly and frequently, kiss and hug each other. They declare their love for each other. Arun even goes to the extent of being ready to marry her. Being a helpless girl, Nur has no courage to convert herself into a Hindu. She, therefore, suggests to Arun to become a Muslim in order to marry her. Thus their love remains pure and unaffected by the communal disturbances happening around them.

But Munir, Nur's brother, suspects that the inter-caste love affair between Nur and Arun may trigger off communal clashes and even endanger the life of Arun. He, therefore, warns Arun to stop seeing Nur and moving about with her. But the young lovers dream of uniting with each other in spite of all the barriers.

The traumatic experience of pyschological separation between Hindus and Muslims is inevitably followed by the physical separation between the two. Politically the border between India and Pakistan has to be fixed. The Hindus of newly created Pakistan have got to leave for the newly created Pakistan. The government appoints a Boundary Commission to decide the precise boundaries of Pakistan and India. Lala Kanshi Ram wishfully hopes that Sialkot may never go to Pakistan. The Sikhs demand and hope that the boundary line will be at the Chenab basin. But Arun knows realistically that the boundary is going to be at the Ravi basin and not at the Chenab. Lala Kanshi Ram and his companions are deeply disappointed by the geographical line of partition. Once the boundary line is decided, the pent up anger and hatred are vented out vehemently and shamelessly everywhere. The Muslims of Sialkot begin to disturb the peace and happiness of the Hindus by stabbing them, looting their houses and shops and raping their women. The life of Hindus becomes utterly miserable and infernal. Although Kanshi Ram has been a harmless merchant, he is deeply upset when his shop is looted by Muslims at night. Lala Kanshi Ram and his Hindu neighbours have to undergo the painful experience of displacement and migration. In spite of their deep emotional attachment to their land, home, shop and region, they are compelled to leave them and go in search of new places for final settlement. The government has arranged many refugee camps to facilitate the process of mass migration from one country to the other. Lala Kanshi Ram feels a terrific anxiety for having to become a landless, homeless and rootless man. He feels an inexplicable agony at having to be severed from his roots :

> Lala Kanshi Ram could not sleep at all that night. It became clear to him how vulnerable the minority community was and that soon he too might have to leave. It hurt him, he thought of it, and he paced his room restively. 'Refugee, refugee, indeed!' he shouted, when he understood the word, 'I was *born* around here, this is my *home* — how can I be a refugee in my own home?'
>
> 'Father, we'll have to leave —' Arun said.
>
> Before he could finish his sentence, Lala Kanshi Ram cut him off. 'Why will we have to? Why?'
>
> 'Well, the government seems unable to protect us, and we'll have to go to save our lives.'
>
> 'Why can't the government protect us? I've seen communal riots before in this country. How were the English able to put them down?'
>
> 'Let's say the government is incapable or unwilling to control the situation. What then? Shall we wait here and perish?'
>
> 'He is right,' said Prabha Rani, fear gripping her heart.
>
> 'Aha! Incapable or unwilling — which precisely?' Lala Kanshi Ram ignored his wife and addressed himself to his son : 'If unwilling, the government is party to murder. If incapable, we Indians had no right to ask for freedom' (p. 124).

Lala Kanshi Ram is so sorrow-stricken that, in spite of himself, he begins to cry. "His eyes filled with tears as he felt so unprotected and forlorn" (p. 125). In spite of the pressure of the members of his family, he is so reluctant to leave. "Lala Kanshi Ram refused to accept his family's suggestion that they pack and leave. How could he leave? He would rather die here" (p. 125). He further worries about his future destiny and place of settlement. Whereas his displacement is certain, his relocation is not known exactly. Everything appears to be bleak and uncertain to him :

> He was young, though, he was only fifty, he could start a business somewhere else, in some town on the other side of the border. But *could* he? Could he, really? He looked at his wife and Arun, and he knew how tired his arms and shoulders were. You mean, to begin right from *scratch*? Wasn't that asking a little too much — now *wasn't* that asking a little too much of a middle aged man? And where precisely would he begin? In what city? How much capital did he have in cash? How early, at how short a notice, could he withdraw it from the bank? What of the shop — the grain stored there? How would he dispose of it? Would anyone give him any price for it in such times? 'Arun's mother, I'm an *old* man and I cannot begin all over again' (p. 126).

Lala Kanshi Ram's worry is not merely about the immediate practical difficulties that he has to face but about his deep seated emotional entanglement with his roots :

> No, that was not all — that was nothing; that was only a small part of the whole story. The pinch was he should have to give up this land, this earth, this air. That's where the hurt lay! He breathed deep filling his lungs with the air of the town to their utmost capacity, and tears welled up in his eyes. How could he give this earth up? (p. 126)

Lala Kanshi Ram feels crestfallen and grows pale. He is forced by the circumstances to leave Sialkot. His good friend Barkat Ali who thinks of Lala Kanshi Ram's safety advises him to leave the town. But Abdul Ghani, the fanatic Muslim enjoys the sight of Lala Kanshi Ram's plight. The communal disturbances continue in the city. The Hindu Deputy Commissioner is shot dead by his Muslim bodyguard. Compelled by the insecure atmosphere, Lala Kanshi Ram decides to leave his house and move to the Refugee Camp. Consequently all the members of his family like Prabha Rani and Arun and his neighbours like Bibi Amar Vati, Suraj Prakash, Sunanda, Padmini and Chandni etc., accompany him in the truck which takes them to the Refugee Camp. Mukunda's mother refuses to go with them and creates a scene. Bill Davidson brings two trucks in the evening and transports them to the Refugee Camp. Thus the process of Lala Kanshi Ram's dislocation has started. He has become totally homeless and rootless and forced to undergo the experience of insecurity and uncertainty.

Lala Kanshi Ram is given a separate tent for his family in the Refugee Camp. But he cannot live peacefully even there. His sorrow is aggravated by the news that his daughter Madhu Bala and her husband are killed by the Muslim fanatics in the train when they are returning to Sialkot. Sorrows keep crowding in in Kanshi Ram's life. His tragedy paradoxically provides a fine comedy to Abdul Ghani who says : 'I'm one of the Khaksar volunteers sir, helping to keep our city clean by cremating the kafir dead' (p. 177). He further expresses his communal hatred :

> And cynically, showing his teeth which lit up eerily in the light of the fire he had said to Arun : 'Who told you your sister was killed, my boy? But don't worry. I put her and her husband into the fire with my own hands, and they're now on their way to dozakh, to hell — where I hope they rot for ever!' He made no effort to disguise his venom (p. 177).

Barkat Ali who is a good Muslim and a friend of Lala Kanshi Ram takes Abdul Ghani to task. But it is of no avail. Kanshi Ram, Prabha Rani and Arun are really heart-broken about the unexpected and premature death of Madhubala and her husband. Their friends try their best to console them. Arun nostalgically remembers his affectionate and almost incestuous relationship with her.

In addition to Lala Kanshi Ram's personal tragedy, he has to bear the public tragedy also happening around him. The communal riots and murders do not cease in spite of the governmental effort o maintain peace in the region :

> What in the end broke Lala Kanshi Ram's heart was the inability of the Boundary Force under General Rees to maintain peace in the province. An Englishman unable to keep law and order! Lala Kanshi Ram reeled when he thought of it. It was like the sun rising in the West. He soon saw how helpless Rees Sahib was though. Most of

> his men and officers were Indians, and they had their separate communal loyalties. These loyalties were openly and unashamedly expressed, and Lala Kanshi Ram heard innumerable accounts of how the minorities in East Punjab and West Punjab were slaughtered while men of the Boundary Force looked on. In such a vicious atmosphere, what could one or a few Englishmen do?
>
> That brought Lala Kanshi Ram to the end of his hopes. Desperately he looked around, desperately he searched his mind, if there was something else he might hang on to. There was nothing. The two new governments were parties to the fratricidal war, and how could unarmed men and women withstand organized slaughter? The death of Madhu was the last blow to his shattered psyche. He now did not want to consider the possibility of staying (pp. 204-205).

Although Kanshi Ram has undergone the traumatic experience of displacement, humiliation and despair, he tries to bear it with a sense of dignity and nobility. He grows more and more withdrawn but never gives up his regular prayer. Perhaps his deep faith in religion and past karma helps him keep his mental balance. In the Refugee Camp, Lala Kanshi Ram and his family have to live on the dry ration supplied to them by the government.

While they are staying in the Refugee Camp, Arun happens to meet his classmate Rahmat Ulla Khan who has now become the army officer and who professes his loyalty to Pakistan openly. Rahmat Ulla Khan treats Arun with tea and drinks and exchanges amicabilities with him. He impresses Arun as a lover and an admirer of Ghalib's poetry. But Arun is shocked and angered when Rahmat Ulla Khan asks him to bring Sunanda, a beautiful married lady, to his bed. Arun realises with discomfort how the partition has created a wall between the Hindu psyche and the Muslim psyche. He excuses himself without any promise to Rahmat Ulla Khan. Later Rahmat Ulla Khan visits the Refugee tent to attract Sunanda's attention to him, but is simply ignored by her. But Rahmat Ulla Khan cherishes a hope of having sex with her sooner or later.

While staying in the Refugee Camp, Lala Kanshi Ram has to see many happy and unhappy natural events taking place around him. For example, Sardar Jodha Singh dies after a brief illness of diarrhoea and is cremated quietly by his family. The Sikhs experience a special threat by the Muslim population. They, therefore, resort to shaving their beard to hide their identity and for safety. They renew their faith in Sikh religion especially in Guru Maharaj. In spite of all these disconcerting events happening to and around them, Lala Kanshi Ram and Prabha Rani maintain a calmness because of their faith in religious fatalism. Kanshi Ram wonders at how religion created by man for the betterment of life in general has degenerated into mad communalism. He broods over the human folly in a philosophical fashion. Having been reconciled to his tragic lot, Kanshi Ram decides to leave for the next place *i.e.* Dera Baba Nanak in the truck. He is made the leader of his group. By this time another tragedy happens around him. Niranjan Singh who cannot face the harsh reality of dislocation and humiliation, sets fire to himself and dies. They conduct his cremation ceremony with great sorrow and proceed with their march ahead.

When they leave the camp, the Muslims jeer at the Hindu men and women and shout insults. Captain Rahmat Ulla Khan hands over charge of the convoy to Major Jung Bahadur Singh. Sufficient military protection is given to the refugees until they leave the camp. While Lala Kanshi Ram is leaving along with his family and neighbours, a shocking event takes place. Gangu Mull, Amar Vati's husband refuses to leave Sialkot as much because of his attachment to his property as because of his dislike for his wife : "You know what a bitch she is — foul mouthed and always quarreling. I was sick of her as it was" (p. 265). He further tells Lala Kanshi Ram : "I'm also thinking of taking a Muslim wife" (p. 265). Amar Vati initially laughs at her husband's absurd decision, but is finally crestfallen by his betrayal. Bibi Amar Vati who was like a lioness once upon a time, has now become helpless like a beaten warrior. Political partition has created a matrimonial partition also in Amar Vati's life. Lala Kanshi Ram has to bear with other unhappy events. He learns that Mukunda's mother has been killed and that "a mass killing of Hindu prisoners did take place inside of the city prison" (p. 269).

They pass the Ramlila ground of Sialkot and march for six miles and halt at Gunna Kalan. Chaudhri Barkat Ali and Munir have walked six miles along with Kanshi Ram's family. Now comes the time for final separation of life-long friends. All separation is painful :

> 'Khuda hafiz, brother Kanshi Ram,' he said, folding his hands.
>
> 'These have been good years,' said Lala Kanshi Ram, taking Chaudhri Barkat Ali's hands in his own.
>
> There were tears in the eyes of both men.
>
> They had nothing more to say, having exhausted themselves of emotion in all these weeks.
>
> 'You took a lot of trouble for us.'
>
> 'Now brother Kanshi Ram!'
>
> Facing Prabha Rani, Chaudhri Barkat Ali said, 'Sister, khuda hafiz.'
>
> 'If not in our life-time, Insha-Allah in the life-time of our children this folly will surely be undone,' said Chaudhri Barkat Ali, looking at Lala Kanshi Ram. 'We are one people and religion cannot separate us from each other' (p. 271).

Munir also says goodbye to Arun and embraces him. Arun knows that the partition of the country has put an end to his love affair with Nur. After thus being painfully separated from the dear friends, Lala Kanshi Ram and his family wait at the open fields outside Gunna Kalan to pass the night. The whole camp hears of the horrible communal atrocities inflicted on Hindu population of Sialkot by the Muslims :

> A number of abducted Hindu and Sikh women were in their custody. Many of the kidnapped women disappeared into private homes. A lone Muslim dragged a woman away, and kept her for his own exclusive use. Or he took her with the consent of other Muslims, converted her to

> Islam, and got married to her. The rest were subjected to mass rape, at times in public places and in the presence of large gatherings. The rape was followed by other atrocities, chopping off the breasts, and even death. Many of the pregnant women had their wombs torn open. The survivors were retained for repeated rapes and humiliations until they were parceled out to decrepit wrecks — the aged, the leftovers who couldn't find a wife, or those Muslims who wanted an additional wife. In the meantime more women were abducted and the cycle was repeated all over again (pp. 289-290).

The whole camp grows dumb with shock when they hear the news of variegated atrocities practised by the Muslims on Hindus. The climax of communal hatred and meanness could be seen in the parade of naked women forced by the Muslims at the bazaar of Narowal in the afternoon. Suraj Prakash and Arun walk upto Narowal to watch the hateful, shameful and grotesque scene. The Muslims of Narowal are dirty, mean, vindictive and sensual :

> The procession arrived. Arun counted them. There were forty women, marching abreast. Their ages varied from sixteen to thirty, although to add to the grotesqueness of the display, there were two women, marching right at the end of the column, who must have been over sixty. They were all stark naked. Their heads were completely shaven; so were their armpits. So were their pubic regions. Shorn of their body hair and clothes, they looked like baby girls, or like bald embryos one sees preserved in mythilated spirit. Only the breasts and hips gave away the age. The women walked awkwardly looking only at the ground. They were all crying, though their eyes shed no tears. Their faces were formed into grimaces and they were sobbing. Their arms were free, but so badly had they been used, so wholly their spirits crushed, their morals shattered, none of them made any attempt to cover themselves with their hands. They swung their arms clumsily, often out of coordination with their legs. The bruises on their bodies showed they had been beaten and manhandled. Their masters walked beside them and if any

> of the women sagged or hung behind, they prodded her along with the whips they carried. At the head of the procession marched a single drummer with a flat drum, thumping heavily on it and announcing their arrival....
>
> The procession moved through the bazaar, and along with the procession moved a river of obscenities — foul abuses, crude personal gestures, spurts of sputum, odd articles like small coins, faded flowers, cigarette butts and bidis that were thrown at the women. As soon as the women came near, that section of the crowd became hysterical. 'Rape them.' 'Put it inside of them.' 'The filthy Hindu bitches.' 'The Kafir women.' Some said worse things. Then came the shower of spittle. Almost everyone spat.... Many men in the front rows of the crowd lifted their lungis to display their genitals to them. Others aimed small articles at them and tried to hit them.... And almost to the last man, whether they spat or shouted or threw things or just stood with their mouths open, they stared at the pubic regions of the women. Through indelicate exposure those areas had lost their glory, lost all magic, and there was only a small slippery aperture you saw there. But men's eyes were settled on these apertures. And the moment the women had passed ahead, the eyes were settled on the bruised buttocks (pp. 292-294).

Though Suraj Prakash enjoys the sight of the parade of the naked women, the good Muslims feel deeply ashamed of their fanatic counterparts. The next night again a large group of Muslims come and attack the Hindu refugees in the camp, with gun-firing. Many Hindus scatter here and there to save their life. Arun also runs away into a nearby field and enters a barn to hide himself for safety. But there he is shocked to see that Sunanda is being raped by Captain Rahmat Ulla Khan. Initially he is not able to identify who is raping whom :

> Arun's heart was beating very fast and he could hear it thumping in his head. Then he heard Sunanda weeping. But it was the weeping of a person drained of all strength, a completely subdued weeping.

> Standing behind the wall, leaning against it with his hands, Arun looked through the passage. First he saw the hay stacked ceiling high is one corner, then he saw a number of farm implements, including a wooden plough, and in the far distance he saw the large, iron door of the barn. It was only then he saw Sunanda or what must be Sunanda. She was lying on the ground on an improvised bed of hay, in the far corner. Her head was away from Arun and he saw her legs. Between her legs and on top of her, was lying a man.
>
> The moonlight was coming through the window in the larger room and Arun could see clearly. She was still weeping. Softly and tamely. Her breath was choked with convulsions. 'Get off me now,' she said in a tired voice. The man did not move. Instead he started laughing. He laughed smugly, a high pitched shrill laughter. The sound reverberated in the barn and the inner door rattled slightly. 'I know I would have you one day,' he said conceitedly. And he laughed again in triumph and satisfaction. 'You are a beauty,' he was saying. 'But you made me wait a long time' (pp. 303-304).

Arun is shocked and exasperated to see that Sunanda is raped by a man. Slowly he recognises that the raper is none other than his own classmate Rahmat Ulla Khan. Righteous indignation surges within him.

> Arun knew who he was before he had spoken. The strong slender back. The tall frame. The familiar sound of the laughter. The shock of it singed him — as recognition shot into him like a leaping flame. He did not stop to think. He did not even know what he was doing. Quietly, step by step, he walked into the other room and picked up a sharp wooden spike from among the farm implements. Step by step, holding the spike firmly in his hands and raising it above his head, he walked to the distant corner. He walked gingerly, as though he were sleep walking at the top of a precipice. He still did not know what he was doing. The spike was raised above his head and his hands were trying to get a firmer hold on it. He made no sound whatsoever, but somehow he did not worry about sound.

> And yet he walked step by step, very carefully. And going near them, while he still heard sobs and the laughter somewhere, he brought the spike down with all his force on the man's head.
>
> He had seen the mass of black hair and he had taken a careful aim. Lying atop her, the man was still holding her in his arms. With the blow his arms slackened and rolled off to the side. His body twitched but the man did not move after that. Arun hit him repeatedly on the head... (p. 304).

Thus Arun's murder of Rahmat Ulla Khan becomes part of wild justice and balance between Muslim hatred of Hindus and Hindu hatred of Muslims. Rahmat Ulla Khan has paid a heavy price of losing his life not only for lusting after a married woman, but also for raping a Hindu woman. Arun consoles Sunanda and tries to help her recover from the sense of being shocked of being raped by a Muslim. Sunanda escapes from the barn along with Arun by dressing himself in Rahmat Ulla Khan's garments. Sunanda requests Arun not to publicise the ugly traumatic experience that has happened to her. She feels that death would have been preferable to the loss of her marital chastity. She sobs and says that, "I should have let him shoot me" (p. 309). Arun takes up Rahmat Ulla Khan's gun and leaves the barn along with Sunanda. He promises her to keep it a secret and takes her back to the Refugee camp.

When both Arun and Sunanda Bala return to the Refugee camp, they are shocked to hear other disconcerting news. Arun is very sad to learn that Chandni has been kidnapped and Suraj Prakash has been stabbed to death by the Muslim sensualists and fantatics. Padmini, Chandni's mother is heartbroken and hits herself all the while in despair. Arun hears about the Muslim atrocities inflicted on Padmini. When the Muslim fanatics came to snatch away her daughter Chandni, Padmini "offered herself to them if they would spare her daughter. But they hit her with a stick and left her unconscious. She also thinks she was dishonoured while she lay unconscious" (p. 315). Arun who loves Chandni searches for her in vain. Padmini goes on waiting and crying for her lost daughter.

On the whole, the refugees are physically and psychologically shattered. When Arun returns to the Refugee camp, he feels terribly depressed. "The women that were discovered were led away silently by their families. None showed joy at the reunion; some seemed sorry the girls had come back at all, soiled and dishonoured" (p. 316). Some refugees were missing. However, the surviving refugees move from Narowal to Dera Baba Nanak. "There was hardly any discipline. There was not a family which had not been hit in some manner, and the refugees were totally dispirited" (p. 316). They continue their march swallowing all the insult and humiliation. "A list of abducted women was prepared, and arrangements were made with the local authorities for their repatriation to India if they were recovered. A list of the dead and the missing was also prepared. And then the refugees started walking the last eight miles of their march" (pp. 318-319). Padmini is reluctant to go ahead until she has recovered her daughter Chandni. Arun worries secretly about his permanent separation from Nur and Chandni. Finally they cross the bridge of the Ravi river and enter the Indian territory. Now all of them have realised that India is their true motherland and wish to greet her. " '*Vande Mataram*,' repeated his father, crushing the earth in his hand and letting it slowly fall to the ground. Arun saw his mother fold her hands and bow to the earth" (p. 320). They develop a religious reverence to Mother India.

Lala Kanshi Ram's family moves swiftly from Dera Baba Nanak to Amritsar. After having suffered from a traumatic displacement, they now have to worry about their relocation. Prabha Rani suggests that they may to Kanpur, or Jullunder, or Ludhiana or Ambala. But Kanshi Ram knows the difficulty of not having close relatives in those cities. "Only now did Lala Kanshi Ram discover the meaning of blood relation. If you were a blood relation, you could shout and force your way in. But, as was the case with them, if you were a distant relation, you could only whine and wait by the outer door" (p. 321). Obviously, Lala Kanshi Ram suffers from a sense of forlornness and unbelonging. But finally he yields to Arun's suggestion of going to Delhi to relocate themselves. Padmini decides to stay on in Amritsar whereas Bibi Amar Vati, Sunanda, Isher Kaur and Teja Singh agree to accompany Lala Kanshi Ram. They are surprised to learn that there is a Sikh/Hindu retaliation for the Muslim atrocities committed in Pakistan. He learns that the people of Amritsar "are taking out a procession of Muslim women through the bazaar" (p. 323). When they go to the railway station, they are shocked to see a train with hundreds of slaughtered Muslims. There is thus a wild balance between Muslim atrocities and Hindu atrocities in the two parts of the nation. Finally they board the train to Delhi. But on the way, the poor Isher Kaur begins to suffer from delivery pains. The womenfolk including a lady doctor from a neighbouring compartment rush to help her. She is, finally, delivered of a female baby in the moving train. Isher Kaur, thus, undergoes a hellish experience in her life. Lala Kanshi Ram is, further disconcerted to see a train accident at Ambala in which ninety-four passengers were killed. When they are passing through the region called Kurukshetra, Kala Kanshi Ram is easily reminded of the Kurukshetra war in the *Mahabharata*. One may easily see a parallel between Kurukshetra war and the modern conflict between Hindus and Muslims.

What is really admirable in Lala Kanshi Ram is that he has developed a philosophical and almost a yogic calmness of vision in spite of all the traumatic experience he and his family have undergone. He knows that Muslims alone are not to be blamed and that Hindus are equally guilty. Although Prabha Rani is very furious with Muslims for killing her daughter, Madhu, Lala Kanshi Ram tries to silence her by his yogic vision : "I can't hate the Muslims any more.... What I mean is, whatever the Muslims did to us in Pakistan, we're doing it to them here! ...We have sinned as much. We need their forgiveness" (pp. 335-336). Lala Kanshi Ram has obviously grown from the worldly level to the yogic level, which helps him to take the future troubles and inconveniences in his stride.

When Lala Kanshi Ram reaches Delhi, he has to face many practical problems of relocation. He meets the Rehabilitation Officer and feels deeply humiliated. He is animadverted for going to Delhi instead of settling down in East Punjab. The Officer treats him rather callously and says, "You have all lost someone!" (p. 338). Lala Kanshi Ram feels terribly depressed and surrounded by darkness. However, swallowing the insult, he pleads meekly, "Sir, I'll be ruined if you don't come to my rescue. I only want a small flat and a small little shop, to be allotted to me" (p. 338). Lala Kanshi Ram requests for a house and a shop *i.e.* Refugee property left behind by the Muslims. The Officer simply laughs at Kanshi Ram's request and directs him to Kingsway Camp. Kanshi Ram swallows all the humiliation silently and takes rest in the Waiting Hall of the Railway Station. He broods about how he has lost everything. He does not know whom to approach at the capital city of Delhi. As the last resort, he decides to meet Jawaharlal Nehru. When he goes to Nehru's residence, he is disappointed to learn that Nehru has gone out of station. His hopelessness is complete now.

Kanshi Ram's companions like Sardar Tej Singh and Isher Kaur find some shelter with some acquaintances in Shahdara, a suburb of Delhi. Although he is happy about their settlement, he suffers from the agony of separation, "It was another bond that had snapped. One by one, he was losing his limbs, and he touched his own arms reminiscently" (p. 343). After separating from these companions, Kanshi Ram goes to the office of the Area Custodian of evacuee property and requests the officer for a refugee flat and a shop. But he is shocked when he is asked to pay a bribe of two thousand rupees for the same. Unable to pay a heavy amount of bribe, he starts searching of a roof above his head. He has become totally 'homeless.' "He wanted a home where he could be alone with Prabha and see his two children" (p. 347). Besides, the people of Delhi are not willing to help Kanshi Ram as he is a Punjabi and tell him to his face that

Punjabis are too quarrelsome. Kanshi Ram goes to the Refugee Office once again and tries in vain to get some shelter. His despair grows so deep that he is on the brink of tears. When Arun enters the office, "His father was stunned to find him there, and he tried to conceal his tears. Had he been weeping? *His* father, weeping openly?" (p. 349). Even the Officer is touched by Kanshi Ram's depth of frustration and advises Arun, "Take care of your people. There is nothing that I can do! There simply aren't any more houses" (p. 349). Arun tries to control his father and takes him to Master Hotel and order for some food. But Lala Kanshi Ram decides to have only tea and biscuits. Observing the plight of his father, even a young man like Arun realises that there is "So much sorrow for a house! Such frustration! Such weariness of the spirit!" (p. 350). Kanshi Ram re-remembers his lost daughter Madhu and suffers from a chasm of pain. Perhaps there cannot be greater tragedy than the one that has happened to Kanshi Ram. He is at the climax of his tragic insecurity, dislocation, rootlessness and homelessness now.

Finally an unexpected surprise awaits Lala Kanshi Ram. When he goes to the Kingsway Camp on Alipur Road, he is happy to find the luxury of living in a brick hutment. "After about four months of irregular living under canvas they found this a luxury" (p. 351). He settles down in the brick hutment along with Bibi Amar Vati and Sunanda. His problem of relocation is finally solved. He begins to adjust himself to the life of Delhi which is full of excitement. To that extent, he feels Delhi to be better than Sialkot. When he slowly begins to strike roots in Delhi, he is disconcerted by the news of Mahatma Gandhi's murder. "When they were playing devotional songs over the All India Radio. A news bulletin came on and it confirmed what the man had told him. It said that Gandhiji that evening had died at the hands of an assassin. He was walking to the prayer meeting from his room in Birla House, when a man approached him and fired three shots. Gandhiji's last words were 'Hey Rama' before he fell. The assassin, the announcement said, was a Hindu. To remove any misgivings, it was repeated the assassin was not a member of a minority community" (p. 355). Lala Kanshi Ram does not pay much attention to the news because of the irreversibility of the sad event and the inevitability of darkness in the subsequent political life of India. "Lala Kanshi Ram heard all that but paid no serious attention to it, though a part of his mind said, wake up, these are good words. Gandhiji was dead — fully dead, competely dead. He found anything after that irrelevant and insignificant" (p. 356). Lala Kanshi Ram, Prabha Rani, Bibi Amar Vati and Arun pay their respect to the late Mahatma by mourning his death by not lighting their ovens and not eating their food.

After a few days, Lala Kanshi Ram starts a small grocery shop to earn his meagre livelihood. Because of all the humiliation that he has suffered in life due to the partition of the country, he has stopped wearing his turban. "It hurt Lala Kanshi Ram no end. From the time he set up this little shop, he had stopped wearing a turban. A turban was a sign of respect, of dignity. He had no dignity left. He now wore of a forage cap. Or he sat bare-headed, advertising his humble position to the world" (p. 359). Like him, Bibi Amar Vati and Sunanda also have grown mellow and tragic. Sunanda acquires an old sewing machine and starts doing odd tailoring jobs.

Lala Kanshi Ram realises the extraordinary importance of political freedom that India has achieved in spite of the horrible and traumatic experiences that he has suffered. "Arun went to the bazaar several times to listen to the radio. Lala Kanshi Ram went with him. For the first time Lala Kanshi Ram became aware of a blessing *azadi* had brought them" (p. 361). Kanshi Ram knows that political freedom and the consequent feeling of security and fearlessness are always preferable to slavery to the British rule. The picture becomes very clear to him when he thinks of the contrast between colonial and post-colonial India. "He thought of the pre-Independence days, before the nation was free. How self-conscious the people were then! An Indian leader dying and the crowd feeling openly for him? It was unthinkable. They sorrowed and they came out on the roads, but there was no dignity in it.

They were afraid of persecution at the hands of the British, they were afraid of violence, they were afraid of their own people who might betray them. And in reaction to those fears, they went into excesses. They wept too loudly or they shouted too loudly. Today the men stood in pride — evenly balanced, firm, sure of themselves. Unlike the past, there was no leader urging them to demonstrate their feelings. The feelings had their own resource. Lala Kanshi Ram raised his head with pride and stretched back his shoulders. He was unrestricted now, he was untramelled" (p. 362). He realizes the extraordinary importance of freedom and emergence of national consciousness in India. He feels proud of himself as an Indian. But his relocation at Delhi has unfortunately severed all his connections and communication with people including his own wife and son. "Lying on his bed late in the night, he thought of it. What of the loss of personality he had suffered? What of the material losses? What of Madhu? That could never be made good, never atoned for. And he saw years of bleakness before him, years of desolation.... He felt himself standing before a tunnel, where he could not see the other end. How long was the tunnel? And it all looked so unnecessary, so superfluous, to him — what they were going through. Freedom was on its way and nothing could have stopped it. If only they had not given in so easily to the partition" (p. 362). He broods over the bleakness and uncertainty of his future. "He wanted to talk about it to Prabha Rani or to Arun. That was another ruin azadi had caused. He had lost the ability to communicate with his family. He couldn't establish a contact either with his wife or with his son" (p. 363). Thus the members of Kanshi Ram's family suffer from a psychological partition from one another and feel unable to communicate mutually. All of them suffer from a sort of existential loneliness. Perhaps all the material suffering like displacement, loss of land, home, roots, friends and relatives, death of his daughter and so on have awakened in him the deep seated Hindu philosophical feeling of *vairagya* or detachment. A member of the Arya Samaj and an ardent believer in Vedic and Vedantic philosophy, Kanshi Ram experiences the essential spiritual loneliness of man and the final encounter with his own self which is part of the Absolute. However, he continues his life in Delhi with a sense of resignation. His son Arun starts going to a local college of Delhi.

Azadi is, thus, an important novel which deals with various aspects of the traumatic experience of partition of the country into two. Chaman Nahal shows his remarkable powers of observation of the human nature in general and the political behaviour of Hindus and Muslims in particular. Though the novel is tragic in its tone, it is epical in its vast canvas. The greatness of Chaman Nahal lies in his balanced and impartial picture of the Hindu-Muslim hatred and love, their emotional and political relationships and the ambivalent relationship between Indians and British people in a very realistic and elaborate manner. The novel is a landmark in the Indian English political fiction providing solid material both to the literary critic and the political psychologist for aesthetic enjoyment and dispassionate research.

NOTE

[All the references to the novel are from Chaman, Nahal's *Azadi* (New Delhi : Orient, Paperbacks, 1979)].

5

The Conflict of Sense and Sensibility in Arun Joshi's *The Strange Case of Billy Biswas*

—*G.A. Ghanshyam*

A crowd flowed over London Bridge so many
I had not thought death had undone so many

—*T.S. Eliot*

IN THIS present century man has become more conscious of his role and responsibility and the psychological impact on his life. He is engulfed with the feeling of loneliness, doubt and value conflict, which are spreading like an epidemic. Edmund Fuller suggests that in our age "man suffers not only from war, persecution famine, and ruin, but also from inner problems...a conviction of isolation randomness and meaninglessness in his way of existence." There is an atmosphere of uncertainty and the modern man is languishing in confusion, frustration, disintegration, disillusionment and alienation. He becomes restless in search for peace and tranquility.

Arun Joshi (1939-1993), an author of rarer sensibility and style, attempts a serious probe into the existential problem and spiritual disturbances of mankind by fixing his focus on certain individualistic characters. His novels demonstrate the edifying lessons of our spiritual heritage that have not been totally irrelevant with the growth of materialism and the rapid Westernization of life in our country. His second novel *The Strange Case of Billy Biswas* is one such probe.

Arun Joshi has placed, both directly and subtly, two opposite forces in the novel. On the one hand, there is the superficial, hallow and materialistic society which represents, and is symbolic of sense, and of consciousness directed by sense. On the other hand, Billy Biswas represents sensibility. He is misfit in society, in the quest for self-recognition and salvation. For him, primitivism is a better "means to an end" than the modern, civilized society. It is a spiritual quest, not for God but for "something like that."

Bimal Biswas or Billy is a man of brilliant intellect, profound sensibility and extraordinary obsessions. He belongs to a rich family, his father being a judge of Supreme Court. Billy was sent to America to take the degree of Engineering but he earns his Ph.D. in Anthropology, because that is his first love. He is deeply interested in the tribal attitudes and customs. On returning to India he feels like a fish out of water and sees no other way out but to fly from the civilized sophisticated modern society. Realizing the shallowness of civilization and the superficiality of its sense of values, both in the United States and in India, Billy Biswas feels himself alienated from society, his friends, his parents, his wife, and partly from his own true nature. Married to an aristocratic convent educated girl, Meena, Billy suffers from the pangs of conscience. The perpetual pricks of his conscience make Billy look strange. There was absolutely no communication between the husband and the wife and their conjugal life turns into the 'most precarious of battle-fields.'[1] This failure to establish meaningful contact with his wife, and with the society she represents only enhances Billy's inner restlessness and his sense of isolation. His cynicism reaches that point that he now questions his girl friend Tuula :

> Why else this constant blurring of reality? Who am I? Who are my parents? My wife? My child? At times I look at them, sitting at the dinner table, and for passing moment I cannot decide they are or what accident of creation has brought us together. (93)

Renouncing his past, his family and the everyday world, Billy Biswas goes in search of a world of meaningful relatedness.

He does not find it either in the white America or in the upper class of Indian Society. He tells his friend Romi Sahai, the narrator of the story, that he had decided to live in Harlem because 'that was the most human place he could find' and that the 'White America was much too civilized for him.' (9) He hates the upper class Indian society swarming with pompous and mixed up people. He sees no other way out but to fly from the civilized world into the saal forests of Maikala Hills to lead the life of the tribal with a view to carving for his soul an inner shrine of tranquility. Romi meets him after a lapse of three years and feels 'as though some part of him had gone on strike.' He ruminates :

> All my words simply sank upon his restless mind without so much as causing ripple. Gone was the staggering intelligence, the spectroscopic interests, the sense of humour. (66)

Billy's disappearance from the face of the Earth into the saal forests of the Maikala Hills is not so much a conscious and deliberate act of withdrawal from society as an attempt to reintegrate himself with nature and primitive people where he belongs. From the very beginning, traces of his love for primitive instinct had been noticed in him. He had run away from home at the age of fourteen, because at that time his slumbering part was awakened and his interest in his own identity was aroused, and he had asked, "Who was I? Where I had come from? Where I was going?" (120). The same sense of belonging in the primitive world was shown when he had gone out with a chauffeur in a village near Bhubneshwar, much against the wishes of his parents. Billy is not aware of his deeper layers. Billy is not quite at home in American society and the civilized life it represents. His itch for India is an itch for deeper things that the primitive aboriginal societies of India represent. Even on his return to India he is not at home in the civilized society and feels like "a visitor from the wilderness to the marts of the big city" (92). The aboriginal life of Maikala Hills in central India becomes a concretization of this worldview and his ultimate rejection of the post Independence, pseudo-western values of his Delhi society to join the primitives and accept their life, thus, turn out to be a symbol of Billy's quest for self-realization and for his identity. Billy's predicament results from his bi-cultural situation. His is the authentic problem of a perceptive young man belonging to the westernized Indian society that has lost its spiritual anchorage. The moral confusion prevailing in the post Independence Indian society is voiced by Billy thus :

> What got me was the superficiality, the sense of values.... I don't think I have ever met a more pompous, a more mixed-up lot of people. Their idea of romance was to go and see an American movie or to go to one of those wretched restaurants and dance with their wives to a thirty-year old tune. Nobody remembered the old songs, or the meaning of the festivals. All the sensibility was gone. So was the poetry. All that was left was loud-mouthed women and men in three-piece suits dreaming their little adulteries.... (176-177)

The absence of primitive world and nature make him feel unhappy and lonely. He needs someone who can share his thoughts, who can respond to him, who can apply a balm to his injured and tortured self. He gets drawn to Rima Kaul and his trips to Bombay bring him close to her. For Billy Rima is an embodiment of that empathy which Meena lacks. Later Billy realizes that mere sympathy cannot reveal his identity. Billy now feels that no woman's body of this phony society can satisfy him. Billy feels that his soul responds to the voices of the hills, forests, untamed nature and the tribal people. He feels happy in the forest because of "the earth, the forest, the rainbows, the liquor from the Mahua, an occasional feast, a lot of dancing and love making and more than anything else, no ambition, none at all" (146). His embrace of primitive world is a part of the maturation of his independent being when he estranges himself from his family and the humdrum world, and begins to realize his own self. This was, what he often talked of, "a great attempt of man to find himself." He refuses to accept clothes, symbolizing civilization, from Romesh Sahai. He takes the death of his mother, and Rima Kaul, his girl friend and the miserable condition of his family in the stride, with total calmness.

In Bilasia, the tribal beauty, Billy finds the right woman who can enliven his soul. Meena deadens his senses; Rima corrupts him and the material civilization kills his innate natural instinct. H.M. Prasad rightly observes :

> It is Bilasia who causes explosion of senses — the proper medium to reach soul. Billy renounces the civilized world and its symbols in Meena and Rima. From Meena to Rima and from Rima to Bilasia is not a mere trifling in Billy's life, it is a development from sex to sympathy and from sympathy to sublimation.[2]

In his interview with Purabi Banerjee, Arun Joshi says, *The Strange Case of Billy Biswas* "is about a mystical urge, a compulsion which makes Billy go away.... In a number of Indian legends and religious texts people go away to forests to heal themselves spiritually. Possibly that's what he is suggesting though not consciously."[3] The novel depicts a metaphysical quest and is concerned with a deeper exploration of the human soul. The vision that haunts Billy in the novel has haunted the seers, the mystics and the visionaries in all ages and in all countries. It is the similar urge that leads Matthew Arnold's Scholar-Gipsy to flee from civilized society with its innumerable ills to the company of primitive community. The story mediates between New Delhi and Maikala Hills, between two distinctly identifiable cultures that these two geographical locations embody. The juxtaposition, and also the conflict, of these two cultures reveal the spiritual uprootedness of the Indian upper crust and the utter falsehood of its superficial glamour and refinement. *The Strange Case of Billy Biswas*, in a sense, is a struggle between two antithetical cultures and attitudes to life. The antagonistic relation between man and his environment is reflected in the plot of the novel that derives its dramatic tension from a confrontation of two conflicting forces. Since the conflict is more of a psychological nature, the protagonist, Billy Biswas, is presented in his own inner struggle. Mathur and Rai aptly remark that *The*

Strange Case of Billy Biswas is a fictional representation of the "universal myth of primitive in the heart of man ever alienating him from the superficial and polished banalities of modern civilization."[4]

Billy is a stranger to the civilized world, and not the tribals. The civilized men are estranged to him. He has an intense hatred for them. He has no love lost for the modern civilization. Like Wordsworth of 'the world is too much with us' Billy feels that this civilization is a monster. It is not a civilization but degradation. He hates the world because it "hangs on this peg of money." He is drawn to Tuula because she has no hankering after money. So is his Bilasia. Billy knows that he is a pilgrim and primitivism will lead him to his goal. "Becoming a primitive was only a first step, and means to an end. Of course, I realized it only after I ran away. I realized then that I was seeking something else. I am still seeking something else" (187). Billy is like those saints of India who want to realize unity with the divine through awakening of their senses. Like the Sadhakas of Tantra, Billy hankers after self-realization, the experience of identification with the cosmos, the divine. For him Bilasia is *Prakriti* and he is *Purush* (male) and the cosmic hole can be experienced in their union. Like an Indian seer, Billy has experienced God-hood. Dhunia, the tribal head thinks that Billy is incarnation of their last king. When he goes to Chandtola with Bilasia, the place begins to glow as predicted by Devi Ma. Dhunia tells Romi that :

> Billy is like rain on parched lands, like balm on a wound. These hills have not seen the like of him since the last of our kings passed away. (157-158)

Romi, the only link from civilization that Billy keeps, turns out to be his betrayal. Romi tries to protect him from the recalling arms of civilization, but things get beyond his control when, through Romi's wife, the secret of Billy being alive is revealed to Billy's father and wife who are determined to get him back. But the effort to capture him led only to the final catastrophe. Billy dies of bullet wounds and only his ashes reach the civilized world. His strange case is disposed of "in the manner that a humdrum society knows of disposing its rebels, its seers, its true lovers." While the civilized world destroys him, the tribal world seeks to perpetuate the memory of the man-god by offering him a shrine. The death of Billy "should not be taken as the death of an isolationist but as the triumph of his ideals and principles."[5]

The end of Billy's story is, in many ways, akin to that of *The Hairy Ape* by O'Neill. Yank in O'Neill's play is also a "symbol of man, who has lost his old harmony with nature, the harmony which he used to have as an animal and has not yet acquired in a spiritual way."[6] Yank's symbolism extends beyond psychology and philosophy and in a sense to anthropology. Yank shakes hand with a Gorilla and is being crushed by him. He meets a death into his anthropological past. The police in the process of retrieving him from the primitive world kill Billy. His case is disposed off in the only way the civilized world knows. But both Yank and Billy in similar yet varying ways explore the profoundest human dilemma of belonging.

REFERENCES

1. Arun Joshi, *The Strange Case of Billy Biswas* (New Delhi : Asia Publishing House, 1971), p. 81. Rest of the extracts are from the same novel.
2. Harimohan Prasad, *Arun Joshi* (New Delhi : Arnold Heinemann, 1985), p. 58.
3. Purabi Banerjee, "A Winner's Secrets". Interview with Arun Joshi, *The Sunday Statesman*, 27 Feb. 1983.
4. O.P. Mathur and G. Rai, "The Existential Note in Arun Joshi's The Strange Case of Billy Biswas and The Apprentice", *Commonwealth Quarterly*, 5/17, (Dec. 1980), p. 35.
5. A.N. Dwivedi (Ed.), *Studies in Contemporary Indian Fiction in English* (Allahabad : Kitab Mahal, 1987), p. 313.
6. Harimohan Prasad, *Arun Joshi* (New Delhi : Arnold Heinemann, 1985), p. 61.

6

HomeGrown Tales of Indian Life : Basavaraj Naikar's *The Thief of Nagarahalli and Other Stories*

—Shankar Prasad Singha

IN SPITE of the many misgivings about the value and worth of the Indian English literature, it has, over the years, established itself as an authentic expression of the Indian psyche and the native sensibility. Quite a few scholars and critics dismissed this new branch of literature with utter contempt and predicted its eventual demise.[1] But proving them wrong, it is not only very much alive but shows vigorous signs of vitality. Every year more and more Indian English writers are getting published both at home and abroad, are applauded, are winning awards in competition with the authors whose mother tongue is English. Professor Basavaraj Naikar's *The Thief of Nagarahalli and Other Stories* is a new addition to the evergrowing body of Indian English fiction. This collection of ten stories written over a period of twenty-five years was shortlisted for the Commonwealth Fiction Prize for the Best First Book from Eurasia in 2000. The stories selected in the collection by the author himself try to capture the myriad hues in the complex web of human relationships in the context of Indian reality. In doing this the author moves from the social to the elemental and even the mythical dimensions of human life.

One of the major controversies in the field of Indian English literature centres round the problem of the treatment of authentic Indian reality, the problem of representing the physical and human landscape that is India. The issue is singularly important in the case of fiction because fiction emerges out of and deals with specific reality which is different for each socio-cultural group, whether co-extensive with the political boundaries or not. The point becomes clearer when one compares the works of a West-based Indian writer with those of an India-based writer. A West-based Indian writer faces problems of adjustment with a new culture, suffers a feeling of restlessness because of the conflict between his/her inherited Indian values and acquired Western ways and values. This becomes his/her immediate milieu and this is something that he/she learns from personal experience. When he/she deals with themes within this area one feels a ring of authenticity in the representation of that reality. But in representing Indian reality such writers frequently appear to be dealing with the reality that is constructed by the media — both print and electronic.

But because his/her intimate knowledge of the socio-geographical community and culture to which he/she belongs an India-based writer of English fiction very often presents an authentic picture of India. In such cases the author is not really writing "about India" or for anyone to whom India had to be presented. As Shashi Deshpande states in an interview with Uma Mahadevan Dasgupta — "I am not writing about 'us' so that 'they' can read about this 'other'. I am writing about us for us."[2] In the interview Deshpande claims that she does never exoticise India or the Indian life and naturally "my kind of writing is not marketable in the west." She states categorically that she writes in English exactly the way she would have written if she had written in Kannada or Marathi. In other words, she merely uses English creatively as a medium to represent the Indian reality and does not subscribe to the view that anyone who writes in English has to write "about India." Of course, representing Indian reality in itself cannot be the criterion or guarantee of aesthetic value. But this provides the solid bedrock, which is carved artistically by the author's creative qualities. Creativity cannot flourish in vacuum.

Naikar's stories are firmly rooted in the Indian milieu and the narrative method he uses in them is redolent of the Indian cultural ethos. The first and title story of the collection depicts the life and exploits of Malla, a (in) famous thief of Nagarahalli, a small village situated thirty-five miles away from Dharwad. Incidentally, Shashi Deshpande who grew up in Dharwad describes the place as "a small town with a very distinct personality."[3] Anybody who reads Naikar's story will be struck by the details with which he establishes the geographical identity of Nagarahalli catching thereby its 'distinct personality.' After trying his hand in many odd jobs Malla settles down at Nagarahalli and becomes an expert thief. The village leader, Marigouda offers him shelter and cunningly reaps the benefit of Malla's thieving. A bachelor, Malla had many myths rumoured about him including even that of an illicit relationship with the Gouda's wife and daughters. But the narrator just hints at this dimension of Malla's character while his attention is devoted to the depiction of Malla's achievements as a thief. Indeed, Malla's greatest pleasure seems to lie in thieving without being caught. He takes great pride in his extraordinary skill in the art and the Gouda just cleverly exploits this sense of pride in Malla to fill his own coffers. Thus one day when Malla gets ready for his expedition to Morab where a dead body had been decorated with countless golden ornaments, the Gouda laughs at Malla's foolhardiness. He wonders how Malla could rob a dead body, which is obviously surrounded by relatives. Malla takes it as an insult to his mastery in the art of thieving and feels secretly irritated. Malla, therefore, took it upon himself as a challenge and ultimately proved his efficiency by playing a trick on the relatives of the dead women. With great diligence he burrowed a hole in the wall exactly behind the dead body of the woman and then inserting his hands into the hole he made the dead body clap twice. In the darkness of the night the terror-stricken relatives thought that the corpse's ghost had returned to the body and naturally everybody fled leaving the dead body all to itself. Malla thus with his wit created the opportunity and divested the dead woman of all the ornaments. Anyone familiar with Saratchandra Chattopadhyaya's short stories will be immediately reminded of a similar situation in his story entitled *Lalu.* Other expeditions of Malla include his stealing of the pitcher with golden ornaments from Desai's house at Annagiri and the golden bowl from the prayer room of the landlord of Imrapur. In both cases through his tricks Malla befools everybody including even a Police Inspector. But on the last occasion Malla is duped by the clever village carpenter Monappa who stole the bowl from the secret place where Malla hid it. Malla came to know it but thought this beneath his dignity to poet it back either by force or through persuasion. On the contrary he threw out the challenge that he would steal it from Monappa. But this time Malla faced more than a match for him and tasted defeat for the first time in his life. It was a humiliation for him but he appreciated the tenacity and alertness of his opponent and left the bowl with Monappa after saluting him with folded palms. The next day he left Nagarahalli and "nobody knew where he had gone and what had happened to him."[4]

The story as a product of conscious artistry has a unity of impression. The author focuses on a single character. Although there are three episodes, they are thematically of a piece with the narrative because all of them only establish Malla's extraordinary skill in stealing. The narrator has resisted the temptation of delineating the amorous aspects of Malla's character, which have been just suggested. The moment of crisis, "the moment at which he undergoes a decisive change in his attitude and understanding"[5] occurs at the end of the story. A man intoxicated with perpetual success he suddenly realizes himself as a creature driven and derided by vanity. This realization, a sort of an epiphany, brings about the fitting finale to the life of a man who was a much talked about figure in the villages of Dharwad taluka. Naikar's narrative method consists of suitably alternating first and third person viewpoints, enabling the reader to understand the character from inside as well as outside. This is the narrative style that Naikar follows throughout with admirable success.

The second story *All for Gold* skilfully blends in its intricate pattern religiosity and amorousness, conjugal love and extra-marital passion, friendly loyalty and betrayal, roguery and simplicity, mercy and revenge. The story opens on the day of the car festival of the village God Lord Kalmeswara. With a careful eye to the details Naikar revives the festival atmosphere in the first few pages with a remarkable success. It is during this festival that Sangappa, the son of the wealthy landlord, is struck by Cupid's arrow on seeing the fascinating contours of the buxom beauty Ganga who happened to be the wife of Virabhadra, a well-to-do businessman of the village. In a state of utter infatuation he first engages his friend Balappa to act as a go-between and persuade Ganga to accept him as her paramour. When Balappa failed in his mission Sangappa employs corner-house Paramma to do the job for him and promises her a golden necklace of five *tolas*. It is this promise of the necklace that makes Paramma act as a procuress. She ultimately tricks Ganga into a trap when she had to agree to receive Sangappa once during the absence of her husband who had been away at Bellary on some urgent business. But what began as a sexual favour conceded under pressure soon turns into a much sought-for pleasure : "As days went by, Ganga not only wanted to forget her husband but secretly even wished his absence from home to be delayed further" (p. 50). Meanwhile one night Virabhadra Setty suddenly comes back from Bellary and catches the two lovers red handed. Ganga is immediately sent to her parents while Setty avenges himself on Sangappa by getting him murdered through hired goons. Ironically, he employs Balappa to win the trust of Sangappa to come to a remote place in the village where he is hacked to death. The story is firmly rooted in the Indian soil depicting the rural life through its various activities and festivals. Naikar handles the psychology of Ganga with considerable skill showing how a married woman with traditional outlook gradually gets into the prohibited pleasures of an extra-marital relationship. Virabhadra's reaction is true to the rural ethos of a patriarchal society where women are considered to be possessions of the husband. His first concern was with his social prestige and it is for this that he could not spare Sangya. Even at the time he was about to axe Sangya, he momentarily felt pity for the man but the thought of his own family honour hardened his heart. When Sangappa fell at Virabhadra's feet and implored him to save his life, "Virabhadra Setty seemed to be touched by the cuckolder's pathetic condition. For a moment he thought of sparing his life.... Immediately Setty remembered his own social prestige and boiled with anger" (p. 58). The story is also given a very telling title in that all the complication and misfortune really culminated with the procuress Paramma agreeing to Sangappa's proposal just for a piece of golden necklace.

The third story begins with the description of a Hindu marriage festival. Naikar really writes for "us" and not for "them" who can read the "other." To respond to a situation like the Hindu marriage ceremony and understand the details and their relevance to the Indian social context a reader has to bring his acquaintance with such rituals. It is thus a situation where the reader constructs the meaning as he reads the story. In fact, without an understanding of the caste-system and the rituals related to the wedding ceremony it is impossible to understand why Girija could not go to her husband, Rajasekhar's house immediately after the marriage; why she had to wait for the auspicious *muhurtam* for *Sobhana.* The tension, the sense of novelty and excitement in the minds of the newly wedded couple is drawn with skill. The family went ecstatic at the news of Rajasekhar's being selected for the Ph.D. programme at Princeton. But then comes the change in Rajasekhar who secretly marries an American girl and decides to settle there. He secured the signature of Girija on divorce papers on the pretext of arranging visa for her. Against this fickleness and treachery of Rajasekhar, the character Girija shines with the traditional Indian virtues of loyalty and constancy. When her mother thinks of arranging her re-marriage Girija calmly answers : "I'll not marry again.... Doesn't matter even if he has let me down so meanly. My parents-in-law are like gods to me. I'll live as their daughter-in-law" (p. 77). Naikar rightly points out the importance of family bonds, which tie people together. Marriage here is not merely an agreement between two individuals but an institution involving two families and the society at large. And it is important to note that Girija's mother secretly felt happy to hear her daughter's resolve although she herself broached the proposal of Girija's re-marriage.

Conceived against the backdrop of the Indian mythical belief in predestination the next story *Mother's Husband* presents a rather macabre account of incest. Setavi, the celestial scribe engraves on the foreheads of the skulls of yet-to-be born human beings their fate according to the Law of Karma. Her daughter's future as entered into the Register of Karma indicates that she is going to have sexual intercourse with her own son. With a heavy heart she has to engrave this account as she was told by the Creator of the cosmos that none could change the fate of anybody. Through many strange happenings in her life Setavi's daughter Kamalata becomes a courtesan and shares the bed with her own son, Adivesha, without knowing his identity. As a result she becomes pregnant and gives birth to a son. But one night she had a horrible dream in which a woman told her that she had slept with her own son and got a son and a grandson at the same time. It was a horrendous knowledge and she could no longer bear the thought. The only course open to her was death and she jumped into a well tucking the baby tightly around her chest with her *sari.* The story reminds one of the Oedipus myth but the author has to realize that what appeared plausible at a bygone age does not seem at all convincing in the twentieth century. There are so many loose ends, which detract from its probability.

The contrast between the inner and the outer man is explored in *The Invisible Face.* The narrator, Mr. Patil who is a close friend of Bangarasetty, the famous merchant of Dharwad, realizes only at the end of the story the difficulty, rather the impossibility of seeing through the social mask. All his life he had known Bangarasetty to be an honest and upright man who was the President's Award Winner. Little did he suspect that

Bangarasetty was in the illegal business of printing fake currency. His accomplices included a minister, a legislator, two other merchants and a landlord. It is they who bribed the Civil Surgeon Deshpande to give poison-injection to Setty when he was really recovering at the Civil Hospital. When the narrator hears this account from Mr. Desai he comes to realize the mysterious behaviour of Deshpande who was a friend of his. Deshpande initially behaved with him very cordially and sincerely tried to save Setty's life. Then when Setty was about to recover he suddenly collapsed and this time Dr. Deshpande's behaviour was very cold : "I was stunned by the doctor's words. There was something unexpected in the tone" (p. 107). After hearing "the whole story" (p. 109) from Desai, the narrator understands the strange behaviour of the Civil Surgeon. The story gives a true picture of the politician-criminal-businessman nexus in the Indian social life laying bare the duplicity that perpetuates the system.

In *She Wanted a Child* Naikar deftly portrays the agony of a woman who is incapable of bearing a child. The instinct of motherhood was quite strong in Manjula and added to that was the social stigma attached to sterility. Manjula therefore desperately needs a child. When she gets a job at Dharwad Manjula enters into an adulterous relationship with her colleague Shekhar only for the sake of getting a child : "I want to have a son by you, Shekhar", said Manjula. "Shekhar was shaken for a moment. 'Why do you want to complicate the matter, dear'?" The reactions of the two are perfectly normal. For Manjula it is a question of getting rid of a social stigma whereas for Shekhar it is merely the pleasures of sex. Even after three months of such relationship when Manjula did not conceive, she went to a gynaecologist and came to know that she could not become a mother without an operation. It is after this that she steals a baby from the Civil Hospital under the guise of a nurse. Finally she is arrested and imprisoned. In this story Naikar predominantly employs the method of 'showing' rather than of 'telling' and the characters reveal themselves mostly through their actions and conversations while the narrator intervenes very sparingly. Thematically as well as from the point of view of style it is quite an enjoyable story.

The next story *When the News Came* provides a humorous account of the confusion arising out of mistaken identity. Chennappa of Navilur is a truck-driver working for a Seth and he goes on a business trip to Belgaum for a week or so. But there is another driver by the same name that hails from Kavalur. The truck-driver Chennappa of Kavalur dies in a road accident but constable Patil of Savadatti Police Station mistakenly enters into the register the name of Chennappa of Navilur. This wrong information is sent to Chennappa's house at Navilur and his wife and son are brought to the police station but as the dead body was smashed to a flat mass of flesh they could not identify it. The burial is arranged at the police station and after that Channappa's wife and son returned to the village. In the meanwhile after some fifteen days Chennappa returns to his village at dusk and the villagers mistaking him for a ghost fled from their homes. Naikar gives a comic description of funny incidents and situations arising out of this confusion. However, ultimately the truth is detected and Chennappa gets re-united with his wife Rudravva to whom are restored vermillion, the bangles, nose-ring and *kumkum*. These details only underscore the true Indian reality especially in the villages. In it Naikar has dealt with the life of a marginalised family in rural India and with a touch of humour brought it alive to the readers.

Coffin in the House really deals with the confession of an elderly bachelor who in a moment of immoderate sexual desire rapes and murders the young daughter of his neighbour. The dead body is kept inside a coffin in his house. Stories like this are occasionally reported in the newspapers and Naikar might have taken his clue from there. But what is interesting is that the character of Mr. Patil is drawn with a good deal of care and sympathy. It only shows man's helplessness against biological instincts and how tragedy occurs because of this. Mr. Patil is not a paedophile or a pervert; he is a normal social man who is by and large liked and respected by his neighbours. That is why when they came to know about the corpse in Mr. Patil's house they did not immediately inform the police. For they thought that it might add to the troubles of Mr. Patil who was recuperating in the hospital after he broke his leg in an accident. They all agreed to Mallikarjuna's suggestion — "I suggest that we all go to the hospital and see Mr. Patil who is a thorough gentleman" (p. 151). Apart from this, the very fact that a young girl was frequently allowed to go to Mr. Patil's house (a bachelor) speaks of the trust that his neighbours had in Mr. Patil. But then suddenly one day he "had an uncontrollable erection and excitement" (p. 154) in his body and in a moment of intense sexual desire he commits a crime which not only lands him in jail but really destroys the man. He feels genuinely repentant for what he had done. When Mallikarjuna says to him in the hospital that the police must be informed about the corpse and the criminals must be punished Mr. Patil says philosophically : "Criminals are punished properly either by the police or by the God" (p. 152). Finally, he asked Mallikarjuna to stay back while other visitors left the hospital so that he could confess his crime. In contrast to the preceding story Naikar here deals with the middle class life in an urban setting.

The next story *The Anonymous Letter* seems to be based on experiences drawn from the author's own life. The narrow-mindedness, jealousy and pettifoggery prevailing in the post-graduate departments in the Indian Universities have been narrated with a genuine insight and skill. Side by side there are descriptions of harmless humour and innocent teasing : "He (Professor Balachandra) turned towards Professor Gangadhar and said smilingly, 'Professor Gangadhar, you look so smart today because of your hair cut. It calls for a celebration.' We all burst into laughter" (pp. 162-63). However the real issue is an anonymous letter written by the MA Final students of Rosegarden University to the Chairman of the English Department. Is it a camouflage for Gulbarga where Professor Naikar began his career? In the letter the students enumerate the complaints against their teachers and want them to address their problems. The charges are very carefully framed and tally, on the whole, with the ground realities in the English Departments in many Indian Universities. I mean that they are typical to a large extent. The likes of Professor Gangadhar or Professor Sekhar may be found in many Indian Universities, particularly the rural ones. Finally it is revealed that the two anonymous letters were written by the students under the instigation of the Head of the Department. The character of the Head of the Department has been very convincingly drawn within a brief span. The Head used to consider the department as his fiefdom and in order to perpetuate his hold on it he did not even hesitate to use the students as pawns in the power-play. That was probably the reality in many universities before the introduction of the rotational system of Headship. A vignette of the campus politics is thus drawn in the story from the inside.

The last one *Fulfilment* is a story of romantic love between Bharati, the only daughter of a retired judge, and Chandrasekhar, the handsome actor of a touring theatre company. Naikar employs the mirroring device in the story where the situation in the play *Jagajyoti Basaveswara* broadly corresponds with the situation in Bharati's life. Bharati first saw Chandrasekhar when he was playing the role of Basaveswara. Among other things, the play dramatizes the marriage between an untouchable bridegroom and a Brahmin bride and the resultant turmoil in the caste-ridden society of Karnataka in the twelfth century. When Bharati falls passionately in love with Chandrasekhar the same situation is re-enacted. Apart from the financial disparity, Bharati was a Brahmin girl whereas Chandrasekhar was an untouchable. But Bharati was not prepared to let these considerations stand in the way of her union with Chandrasekhar. So the two lovers flew to a far-off village and with the help of friends get married there. The forlorn father whose life was really rooted in his daughter took it much to heart. He set out on a pilgrimage to the Himalayas after bequeathing all his property to the Sringeri Math of Sankaracarya. Meanwhile Bharati lived happily with her husband and soon gave birth to a boy. But after three years Chandrasekhar was falsely implicated in a criminal case and a warrant was issued against him. He, therefore, left the place and wandered in disguise for long twelve years when the time limit for the warrant actually expired. After twelve years he came back to his wife and "both of them remained in a paradise of silent sweetness" (p. 193). It is thus a romantic story of an ideal love, which does not wither or get stale with the passage of time. Quite naturally the characters here are really not drawn in the round but they remain the same throughout. It has a charm of a different kind, which does not lie in psychological subtleties.

The ten stories in this collection offer a wonderful variety of themes and experiences gathered from personal experience and direct observation. The author seems to treat with equal ease situations from rural as well as urban life, experiences romantic as well as ironic, characters from the margin as well as the centre of social life. In the process he provides very authentic accounts of Indian life in its myriad diversities. He relies heavily on Indian myths and rituals to present characteristic Indian settings and thus should be considered as belonging to the Nativist tradition. Human relationship or more precisely love-relationship seems to form the staple of many of the stories. Naikar explores human love in all its varieties — from the calmly conjugal to the passionately adulterous. Sexuality obviously has a prominent place in some of these stories. Naikar is quite uninhibited in treating sexual reality but occasionally he seems to have forgotten the virtues of suggestivity. He goes into the details with gusto without being able to fish up sex from the mud into which it has been sunk by the hypocritical and timid Indian middle class. When one compares the description of lovemaking between Sangappa and Ganga in Naikar's *All For Gold* with the one between Paul Morel and Clara Dawes in *Sons and Lovers* the point becomes clear. Naikar has not been able to raise it to the level where sex stands for integration with the cosmic forces. The narrative method broadly oscillates between *diegesis* and *mimesis,* between telling and showing. In some of the better constructed stories there are passages in which dialogue and character interaction give a dramatic effect making the reader forget about the narrator. But nowhere have the two devices become exclusive categories; rather both of them together represent a continuum with minimal narrator colouring at one end and maximal narrator colouring at the other. If the title story displays maximum narator colouring, *She Wanted a Child* represents the minimal. The language sometimes shows the pull of the native speech but that is probably inevitable in a writer who is confined to Indian education and lives in India. The native pull in language and imagery, however, is evocative of the Indian reality and ethos and should not be necessarily considered as a drawback. For no less a writer than Raja Rao pointed out in 1937, "We cannot write like the English. We should not."[6] These home grown tales do not offer an exotic India in a neat package but they are concerned with the homely joys and humble fortunes of a cross-section of the Indian people who come alive in the pages of Naikar's book. And that is no mean achievement.

NOTES AND REFERENCES

1. R.C. Dutt in his *The Literature of Bengal* (1895) declared that "All attempts to court the Muse in a foreign tongue must be fruitless" (p. 185). The famous Bengali poet-critic Buddhadeb Bose wrote in 1963 that Indian English poetry was "a blind alley lined with curio shops leading nowhere." (Stephen Spender and Donald Hall (eds.), Buddhadeb Bose, "Indian Poetry in English", *The Concise Encyclopedia of English and American Poetry,* p. 178). It was in the same year that M. Chalapathi Rau in an article entitled "The Indo-Anglians" published in *The Illustrated Weekly of India* (LXXXIV, 21, 26 May, 1963) opined that "Indian writing in English is at its best composition, and the best part of it is translation. Nothing more is possible except for someone who can live the language, think the language and write, not compose in the language" (p. 45). Much the same view has been expressed by a senior academic even in 1991. Professor Bhalachandra Nemade in *Indo-Anglian Writings : Two Lectures* (Dharwad, 1991) dismisses the entire body of Indian English literature as "tourist fiction" and predicts that it will wither away when a well-planned programme of translations from the regional languages is undertaken. Even Uma Parameswaran who herself writes in English, in her *A Study of Representative Indo-English Novelists* (1976) proclaims that Indian English literature was dying and with an uncanny

precision fixes the year of death to be 2000 AD (p. 6). For some of the details I am indebted to M.K. Naik's "Towards the New Millennium : Indian English Literature Today" in *The Journal of Indian Writing in English,* Vol. 9, No. 1, January 2001.

2. "Interview", *The Sunday Statesman Literary Supplement,* Kolkata, 13 May 2001.
3. *Ibid.*
4. Basavaraj Naikar, *The Thief of Nagarahalli and Other Stories* (Calcutta : Writers Workshop, 1999), p. 27. All subsequent quotations are from this edition and page references are shown in the body of the text.
5. Ian Reid, *The Short Story* (London : Methuen, 1977), p. 56.
6. Raja Rao, 'Foreword' to *Kanthapura* (1938; Delhi : OUP, 1998).

7

The Silent Women : A Study of the Position of Women in *The Thief of Nagarahalli and Other Stories**

—*Aroonima Sinha*

THE THIEF of Nagarahalli and Other Stories is a collection of short stories by Professor Basavaraj Naikar of the Karnatak University, Dharwad. The preface of the book avers that the ten stories included in the book were written at different periods of time and deal with various aspects of human relationships in our life. The stories certainly deal with a vast range of emotions and situations from "the social to the mythical and elemental dimensions of life."[1] Written in the author's own inimitable style, there is an earthy quality in all the stories. The characters of the stories are people who with their lively interaction "enlarge a moment and unravel a situation in all its nuances"[2] to bring out the contradictory traits inherent in human nature.

The characters in the stories are rural or small-town people. In his choice of characters one is reminded of R.K. Narayan's unforgettable Malgudi characters, who within their limited range of functioning, exhibited the entire range of human emotions. But Naikar's characters, unfortunately, are not so finely chiselled as those of Narayan's are. This is because of his obsession with sex, various forms of seductions, guilt consciousness and repentance. This gives the stories a typical farcical and melodramatic flavour

* Shortlisted for the Commonwealth Fiction Prize for the Best Book from Eurasia in 2000.

often to be found in folklores and 'Gathas' of India, where the situation often overshadows the characters.

The paper, however, intends to analyze the position of women in *The Thief of Nagarahalli and Other Stories* and through this endeavour study the effect of changing values in their status. This is rather difficult because there are only a few female characters that merit attention. But they are certainly more memorable than their male counterparts. As stated earlier, all these female characters are rural or small-town women who act and think in accordance with their social milieu. Most of them are victims of circumstances, of social and traditional bindings, while others are victims of their own passions. None of the women, except for one, ever stand up for themselves nor speak for their actions.

Ganga, in the story *All for Gold* is perhaps the most vulnerable of all female characters. The title of the story *All for Gold* is misleading because Ganga's predicament comes not for her love of gold, which is universally accepted as the greatest temptation for women. It is Paramma, another female character whose love for gold motivates her to drag the unprotected Ganga to an ignominious end.

Ganga is a young married lady with voluptuous body who catches the eye of a rich man Sangappa during 'rath-yatra' festivities of Lord Kalmeshwara. She accidentally drops her gold necklace and this becomes a via media for Sangappa to break the ice with her. The story begins with a graphic detail of the intimacy between Sangappa and his childhood friend Balappa who is used cleverly by the former as a pawn in the sordid game of seduction. Ganga, however, rebukes him and takes shelter behind her safe married status. Sangappa, totally disheartened with Balappa's defeat, seeks the service of Paramma, a wily old lady who is avaricious and crafty. She plays the role of a pimp or a shrewd and deft procures only for the sake of a five-tola gold chain. She at first tries to play upon Ganga's vanity by comparing her beauty to that of Goddess Rati and then broaches the subject of Sangappa's infatuation. But Ganga 'cannot be tricked so simply' and insults Paramma. Paramma gets a chance when Ganga leaves her for a little while to attend to the boiling rice. She leaves Sangappa's turban on the string cot in Ganga's room. Later she accosts Ganga as to how Sangappa's turban is to be found in Ganga's house. Ganga is frightened because she knows the repercussion of this. She knows that Paramma, with her old woman gossip, is sure to spread the story and tarnish her reputation. Thus, blackmail becomes the weapon of Paramma and she succeeds where Balappa had failed.

Ganga's predicament can be well understood and she tackles the dilemma in a very pragmatic fashion — though many would say — she takes the easiest way out. She felt "that the only way was to entertain Sangappa that night and request him to keep himself away from her ever after sinning once in secrecy would not be a great problem, she thought. She would be free from all those machinations for good. She, therefore, decided to go through the experience once with Sangappa and be done with it. She began to imagine Sangappa in a new light. She also felt the anticipatory thrill and fear for uniting with a man other than her husband. She felt vibrations all through her body. She began to rationalize things for herself out of her helplessness. She imagined herself in Sangappa's arms. She thought, why not enjoy it with him secretly? Anyway, her husband was away from home. Why not make the best of the golden opportunity?"[3]

Her guilt deserts her when she confronts Sangappa whose 'beautiful mustache'[4] leaves her burning with desire. Then begins their lusty association that leaves Ganga breathless with pleasure. Their erotic cohabitation, so vividly and graphically described by the author in its raw intensity, strives "to show the transcendence achieved by the lovers once they mate with gay abandon, wanting to give and receive simultaneously. The 'I-Thou' dichotomy is dissolved, and the lovers oblivious of every thing including their respective 'selves' get transformed into one entity."[5]

The question, however, is whether the call of the flesh is stronger than the call of moral or social values. Sex has the capacity of transcendence but man can only sample it within social norms. The relationship between Ganga and Sangappa, however "spirit-lifting" it may be, is by social standards, an illicit relationship and both Sangappa and Ganga suffer for it. Ganga is abandoned and Sangappa murdered by Ganga's husband. The character of Ganga would certainly hurt the sensibilities of a large section of our orthodox society. They are accustomed to the pedestal figures of women in literature and would readily censure Ganga as a lose woman. But Ganga is human. She just like Catherine in *Wuthering Heights* elicits our sympathy. Indeed, Ganga and her kind are not rare in society and her succumbing to passion is not an unusual event.

Her Husband Went to America treats the overused familiar situation of betrayal of an innocent wife by a self-centred husband, swept off by the glamour of American life. Girija, an innocent young village belle seems to be a ready victim of circumstances. The ordinary aspirations and dreams of an ordinary woman are all embodied in Girija. Uneducated, she tries to immerse herself into housework and looking after her in-laws while waiting for her husband to come back from America and start together a prosperous life. The lack of education and especially the lack of the knowledge of English, become an albatross around her neck when she unwittingly signs her own divorce papers. Girija's story is a story of betrayal of trust, of innocence versus craft and cunning. Her hurt and trauma can be well understood but she takes everything in her stride. She decides not to remarry, even when her mother persuades her to. Why she does so is not made very clear by the author. Is she wary of the male clan or is she held back by tradition? Girija herself says : "No, mother, I'll not marry again. I have married him and shall remain his wife all through life. Doesn't matter even if he has let me down so meanly. My parents-in-law are like gods to me. I'll live as their daughter-in-law."[6]

Girija chooses to live with dignity and her mother is glad to see that her "daughter had developed the courage to face the unexpected challenges of life."[7] Girija and her situation only corroborates the fact that an Indian male marries only his wife whereas an Indian woman marries the whole family.

Mother's Husband is certainly a very unusual type of story with a mythical background. The author has tried to project another version of the oedipal theme through the device of prophecy. Setavi, the mother of Kamalata is a goddess engaged in the work of writing the destiny of creatures to be born in the future. During one such séance, she writes the future of her own daughter who is yet to be born. The goddess is incarnated and gives birth to a female child. The future of the daughter is devastating. She would disgrace mankind by developing incestuous relationship with her own son. Kamalata, as she is called, is sweetness and beauty personified. In due course she becomes young and wanders away to the woods. She meets her future husband Madappa. There is an instant chemistry working between them and both succumb to passion. Kamalata accompanies her paramour without even asking his name.[8] She does not even think about her widowed mother when she lives with her husband for five years and gives birth to a healthy son. She abandons her husband as soon as she learns about his trade and caste, which is of a cobbler. "She never thought that she had married a cobbler. She went to the backyard and sat under the neem tree brooding over the matter. She cursed herself for yielding herself to him in her weak moment in the wood and letting down her own mother. She felt ashamed of being the wife of a cobbler. She cursed herself again for never having enquired about his family, his background and profession. The sweetness that she had felt between his strong arms and maddening thighs had made her completely oblivious of his caste, profession and lineage."[9]

She becomes a prostitute in Dhawalpura and acquires the name of Chandrasani. She attracts people from all ages and her own son Adivesha, now a young man and jewel merchant, hires her services not knowing that Chandrasani was his own mother. Adivesha is "dazzled by her exquisite beauty. He felt as if the moon had descended from the sky."[10] Though he finds the features of the lady vaguely familiar he shrugs off the feeling concluding that it must be "just a resemblance."[11] Chandrasani too is attracted to Adivesha and admires his : "...glowing cheeks, mischievous mustaches, inviting lips, broad shoulders and sumptuous thighs. Although she had tasted many men, she had never felt so attracted to them."[12]

After their consummation, which the author has described graphically, their "souls were disconnected from their bodies as it were and soared in the sky like two balloons."[13]

Chandrasani or Kamalata soon discovers she is pregnant and after some time gives birth to a son. She is overjoyed but she is told the truth in a dream. After learning the truth she begins to "shake with shame and fear" and with a choking sensation in her throat she asks, "Oh! did I get a grandson and a son at the same time?"[14] She kills both herself and her newborn son by jumping into a well. Adivesha perhaps never learns the truth behind Chandrasani's suicide. The story leaves the impression that a woman is often lonesome in her guilt.

Bharati, in *Fulfilment*, is perhaps the strongest and the best-evolved character in Naikar's book. Belonging to the upper middle class she is a motherless child of an aging, orthodox and religious father. Surrounded by luxuries she remains "unhappy deep in her heart."[15] Naikar has very vividly described the situation of Bharati. She is not allowed to pursue her education after she passes her matriculation and she justifiably feels suffocated in her paternal home. She is trapped with her father who was :

> ...in a sense a martinet and a disciplinarian. Every morning and evening he would unfailingly perform his sanctimonious duties as laid down in the sacred books. Then he would read aloud the *Bhagavad-Gita* and *Gitagovindam* up to lunchtime. After his meals, he would take rest for an hour or two in the afternoon and at about four o'clock in the evening he would go to the old friends to discuss Brahmajnana and other philosophies in the Temple of Iswara. At six o'clock he would return home

> and again perform his daily rites, take his supper and go to bed at about nine o'clock.[16]

She escapes her insipid situation by eloping with a handsome actor called Chandrashekhar. She breaks all class and caste barriers when she, the daughter of a 'retired judge' agrees to plunge all comforts and her social status for a life with an untouchable. Her act of defiance seems to be an impulsive act — an escape from her boring existence. But it is total surrender for Bharati. She soon discovers that life is not a bed of roses. After three years of conjugal bliss, which is obviously sans all the comfort she is used to, she has to part with her husband, who is running away from the police on false charges, for twelve years. She does get him back after twelve years.

Bharati's initial rebellion against class, caste and her poor father is the only factor that lends colour to her character. But subsequently, Bharati is back into the traditional mould of a "Bharatiya-nari" — the long suffering, penance-practicing female waiting patiently for fate to hand out the rewards.

The position of the female characters in Naikar's book is, to say the least, disheartening. None of them exhibit any modern traits. They all seem to be rooted in the bygone eras when women were more or less objects of desires to be used or discarded at pleasure. Ganga, for example, could have rebelled by deserting her husband and going out openly to live with her paramour. But both Sangappa and Ganga cohabit on the sly so that Ganga's married status remains intact and Sangappa does not face problems at home. Girija could have rebelled by marrying again or leaving her in-laws to carve out a separate identity. But she prefers to be the good daughter-in-law, which the latter too must have found quite convenient. Where else could they have got a free hand maiden to look after them. Kamalata too is a woman of confused identity. She feels ashamed and deserts her husband when she learns about his profession and caste, but she does not feel any qualms in adopting the lucrative profession of a courtesan. Bharati, of course, knows what she wants but slips back into the traditional mould and waits for twelve years for her husband to return. None of these women rebel or try to alter their situation. If they do (like Manjula in *She Wanted a Child*, who steals a baby from the hospital to tide over her yearning for a child), they are caught and brought to book. It cannot be denied that these women are prototypes of women still found in a majority of our rural areas and hence their portrayal cannot be called unrealistic. The sweeping changes in the status of women are still a myth for them. Aristotle said that silence was women's glory, and perhaps that is why Naikar's women are so silent and non-aggressive. Like true traditional women they accept life, as it is, not trying to alter the situation.

REFERENCES

1. Preface : *Thief of Nagarahalli and Other Stories*, Basavaraj Naikar, (Writers' Workshop, Calcutta, 1999).
2. Book Review, *The Indian Journal of English Studies,* Vol. xxxvii, p. 141.
3. *All for Gold*, p. 46.
4. *Ibid.,* p. 49.
5. Book Review, *The Indian Journal of English Studies,* Vol. xxxvii, p. 142.
6. *Her Husband Went to America,* p. 77.
7. *Ibid.,* p. 77.
8. *Mother's Husband,* p. 86.
9. *Ibid.,* p. 88.
10. *Ibid.,* p. 92.
11. *Ibid.,* p. 92.
12. *Ibid.,* p. 93.
13. *Ibid.*, p. 95.
14. *Ibid.*, p. 97.
15. *Fulfilment,* p. 179.
16. *Ibid.*, pp. 178-79.

8

Postcolonial Discourse in the Novel of Amitav Ghosh's *The Shadow Lines*

—*P.D. Dubbe*

POSTCOLONIAL DISCOURSE means something that has a concern only with the national culture after the departure of imperial power. Postcolonialism is a state of consciousness, a crucial stage in the continuum of cultural process and self-awareness. It involves two type of Imperialism, Political and Cultural. Therefore myth and history, language and landscape, self and the other are all very important aspects of post-colonialism. Postcolonial theory claims that the major theme of literatures from postcolonial countries can be taken as resistance to the former coloniser. It further assumes that the writers who write back to the centre are representing the people of their society authentically. Postcolonial theory is using terminologies like "The Oppressed", the colonised people and the indigenous to describe postcolonial societies, it suppress internal hierarchies and divisions in these societies.

The theory is not born of an immaculate conception but emerges of the conditions of living. So postcolonialism or postcolonial theory which claims that all literatures from the above mentioned geographical 'share' certain formal and discursive features, which have been identified as 'resistance' and 'subversion' of the imperial 'centre' and can therefore be treated as collectively under the name postcolonial literature. To assume that the word postcolonial encapsulates a unified and homogeneous experience is to disregard the material consequences of colonialism upon which postcolonial discourse is constructed. But to exclude some societies from the term for tawdry motives of political correctness is both to ignore the material effects of colonisation and the huge diversity of ordinary and sometimes hidden response to it throughout the world.

The theme of exile of belonging and non-belonging is a common link between writers from postcolonial cultures. Equally the problematic of language and national identity offers another fundamental point of unity. We are aware of the fact that the term postcolonial is not as precise as one would like, but has always proven difficult to find completely satisfactory nomenclature that would accommodate, for example, the literature of such diverse countries as Canada, Nigeria and New Zealand.

Colonial discourse is associated with the politics of interrelationships as and when they are affected by patterns of authority or subjugation. Looked at from this point of view, it is easy to find strains of political discourse in any test which thematically or otherwise employs the interplay of class, gender or hierarchical relationships.

The term postcolonial in its various usages carries a multiplicity of meanings that need to be distinguished for analytical purposes. The term seems to be especially prominent. As a literal description of conditions in formerly colonial societies, in which case the term has concrete referents as in postcolonial societies or postcolonial intellectuals. As a description of a global condition after the period of colonialism, in which case the usage is somewhat more abstract and less concrete in reference comparable in its vagueness to the earlier term third world, for which it is intended as a substitute. Even at its most concrete, the significance of postcolonial is not transparent because each of its meanings is overdetermined by the others. Postcolonial intellectuals are clearly the producers of a postcolonial discourse, but who exactly are the postcolonial intellectuals? Here the contrast between postcolonial and its predecessor term third world, postcolonial critics insist, was quite vague in encompassing within one uniform category heterogeneous historical circumstances and in locking in fixed positions structurally if not geographically, societies and populations that shifted with changing global relationships.

Amitab Ghosh was born in Calcutta and in his early years witnessed the varied cultural life of Calcutta, Dhaka (Bangladesh), Colombo (Sri Lanka). He graduated from the University of Delhi, before taking his Master of Philosophy in Social anthropology at Oxford University, England. During the Emergency (1975-77) Amitav Ghosh worked as a Journalist with the Indian Express Group of Newspapers. Ghosh seeks to structure his novel '*The Shadow Lines*' with reference to the three cardinal qualities, that according to Indian Philosophy, make individuals what they are, '*Rajas* : *Passion*', '*Satwik* : *Reason*' and '*Tamas* : *Death*', the order indicative of a Soul's gradual and upward evolution. The novel *The Shadow Lines* can be described as the narrator's journey backwards in time, it is an attempt to impose a pattern on experience. The story of the novel emerges in layers and each layer is a fusion of private lives and public events, all linked into a thematic unity.

The novel is divided into two parts, '*Going Away*' and '*Coming Home.*' The novel beautifully shifts from past to present and from present to past, Ghosh manages in a masterly way time of two kinds, time past : memory and time present : reality. The first section '*Going Away*' means '*going away from self*', '*Coming Home*' means '*Coming back in the self.*' The concept of coming and going not belonging more often than the belonging is expressed as part of the family's secret lore because :

> "You see, in our family we don't know whether we're coing or going — it's all my grandmother's fault. But of course, the fault wasn't hers at all : it lay in language. Every language assumes a centrality, a fixed and settle point to go away from and come back to and what my grandmother was looking for was a word for a journey

> which was not a coming or a going at all a journey that was a search for precisely that fixed point which permits the proper use of verbs of movement."[1]

So, one is constantly plagued by doubts in the novel as to whether the characters are going to Calcutta or coming to Calcutta or coming to London or going back to London. The two sections of the Novel clearly indicate this enigma of having to decide where home is Calcutta or Dhaka (Bangladesh) or London. When home is an uncertain place, borders too compound the problem.

The first section *'Going Away'* ends with the narrator's coming face to face Ila's indifference towards him. It also ends on a note that Ila possessed his life and her going, away meant death to him. The second section *'Coming Home'* ends with the narrator's regaining self-possession, his getting over his love for Ila, union with May and acceptance of Tridib's death.

The novel is full of symbolic references to Houses old and new, maps and mirrors, borders and boundaries. All these symbols in one way or the other deal with the theme of man's search for identity, his search for roots. This is not a story of the grandmother but it is a story of the eternal suffering of every man torn between the past and the present. The novel raises serious question about roots, identities, war, borders and so on.

> "I would have been frightened she said. But I would have prayed for strength, and Good Willing, yes, I would have killed him. It was for or freedom. I would have done anything to be free."[2]

These are the words exclaimed by the nameless grandmother. Amitav Ghosh in *The Shadow Lines* about partition and immigration explores man's eternal quest for freedom. He clearly shows that it is not humanly possible to be totally free. One can only attempt it. Though all the characters in the novel exhibit an urge to be 'free' none of them is totally free in the end. 'Freedom' therefore means a number of competing discourses that cannot be mistaken for a single metaphysical state. The impossibility of attaining complete freedom is voiced by the narrator.

> "If freedom were possible, surely Tridib's death would have set me free. And yet; all it takes to set my hand shaking like a leaf, fifteen years later, thousands of miles away at the other end of another continent, is a chance remark by a waiter in a restaurant."[3]

The novel is a powerful adolescent love story and a story of unrequited love. The narrator realises that Ila would never love him as he loved her. Tridib also loved May but May was never sure of her love for him. Nick Price is May's brother whom Ila loved. Ila always pretended that Nick was her knight in shining armour, but Nick betrayed her as a child and subsequently as an adult Ila tries hard to discard her Indianness. She wanted to go to night club in Calcutta where she wanted to drink and dance. Her cousin Robi did not allow her and hurt, she says :

> "Do you see now I've chosen to live in London? Do you see? It's only because I want to be free. Free of your bloody culture and free of all you."[4]

It is surprising that Ila with her upper middle class values marries a person who does not love her and who is a wastrel. It is strange that she just want to skim the surface of life.

The novel tells the story of three generations of the narrator's family spread over Calcutta, Dhaka (Bangladesh) and London and lines up characters from different nationalities, religion and cultures in the world. The grandmother, Jethamoshi, Mayadebi and Shaheb are representatives of the first generation, the Father, the Mothers, Jatin are eccentric representatives of the second generation, Ila, Nick, May and the Narrator are representative of the third generation.

The third situation is portrayed when May and the Narrator lie together in London in 1979, on the eve of the Narrator's return to India. All the three situations are presented specifically after violent happenings in Dhaka. Ghosh portrays violence affected far off places both in Time and Space only to give meaning to love making, the reality of life, force and to show

how Tridib, May and the Narrator grow mature in Understanding and attain redemption through Love. The situations are the same but the players are different. Both May and the Narrator find release from the mystery of Tridib's death a sacrificial offering as May calls it, which cannot be explained or understood.

> "Do you think I killed him? she said. I stayed silent. I did not want to answer her. I used to think so too, she said I though I'd killed him.
>
> I was safe you see. I could have gone right into that mob, and they wouldn't have touched me, an English memberahib but he, he must have known he was going to die.... He gave himself up. It was a sacrifice. I know I can't understand it, I know I mustn't try, for any real sacrifice is a mystery."[5]

In short Amitav Ghosh's work seems to move effortlessly across national frontiers, as Robert Dixon puts it not inhabiting "a culture rooted in a single place, but a discursive space that flows across political and national boundaries and even across generations in time."[6]

REFERENCES

1. Amitav Ghosh, *The Shadow Lines*, Ravi Dayal Publisher, Delhi, 1996, p. 153.
2. *Ibid.,* p. 39.
3. *Ibid.,* p. 247.
4. *Ibid.,* pp. 88-89.
5. *Ibid.,* pp. 151, 152.
6. Rovert Dixon, "Travelling in the West : The Writing of Amitav Ghosh", *The Journal of Commonwealth Literature*, 31.1 (1996), p. 9.

9

Be Your Own Hero(ine) : A Case Study of Sahgal's *Sonali Ranade**

—*Asha Choubey*

> She's a woman who is confident, assured, strong, independent, intelligent, sensual, spiritual, loving, creative, and very much in touch with her feminine side. She has brought the lessons of her past with her and now in this new era, knows exactly who she is, where she is going and what she wants in life. She values family and friends, and believes that women are unique individuals in their own right. She believes in a higher power that exists for our own good and is in awe of beauty in the universe. (http://mistrettastudios.com)

THIS IS how a feminist web site describes the millennium woman. We may have our own vision of her but we do not disagree with the writer here. The millennium woman of our dreams is not only proud of her womanhood but she also makes womanhood proud of her. An interesting element about the image of the millennium woman is that this is an image not created by men and followed by women but as Holland Cotter says : "Women are taking control of their own image making." (http://www.nytimes.com/library/magazine/millennium/m2/cotter.html). The millennium has a long way to go but the nineties have given it initial shape. Women today have a very different approach to life. The Barbie's ads now read : "Dream

---

* This paper was presented at the VI Annual Conference of Indian Association of Studies in Contemporary Literature at B.H.U. Varanasi on 28-29 September 2000.

With Your Eyes Wide Open" and "Be Your Own Hero." This is what today's woman believes in. This has to be the picture of the millennium woman. The millennium woman is not only strong, she knows her mind as well. With her strength she dares to command her circle. She is right herself and also has a right influence over her man.

I

Nayantara Sahgal, a writer who flourished in the seventies and eighties maintains her relevance today as a humanist with obvious feminist concerns. Her early women present that phase of Indian womanhood when the shadow of orthodox notions and of decaying traditions still loomed large on the women-psyche. Discontentment and frustrations were experienced but they seldom led to retaliation. These women are not as much oppressed by men as they are sufferers of their own inertia and reluctance. *A Time to be Happy, This Time of Morning, Storm in Chandigarh, The Day in Shadow* and *A Situation in New Delhi* fall in this category. Sahgal presented her new woman in her very first novel *A Time to be Happy* in the person of Maya. The thirst of her new woman began with Maya's desire for "a response" (Sahgal 1958 : 68) and it continued to display itself in Rashmi's search for "recognition of her existence" (Sahgal 1965 : 78) and in Simrit's wanting "only to be" (Sahgal 1971 : 7). These women however continue to be governed by some men or the other. From Maya to Devi, Sahgal marches decades ahead but this march is more chronological than ideological. Her women from Maya to Devi are much the same in their easy pliability and vulnerability. These are women in chrysalis. It was in the second and hitherto last phase of her career that Sahgal gave a truly emancipated woman in the character of Sonali Ranade in *Rich Like Us.* In the creation of this character Sahgal evinces her prophetic vision in anticipating the woman of the new millennium. This paper attempts to present a case study of Sonali Ranade in order to posit her as the face of the millennium woman.

II

The portrayal of Sonali seems to be the inevitable culmination of Sahgal's feminist vision. In fact, with Sonali we enter into a new era, a new experience in Sahgal's fictional world. Her milieu resembles that of today's woman. She is a daughter as well as a working woman and as such she faces many pressures that women of today face. Daughter of a liberal father she has an orthodox woman for her mother. While Sonali wants to hold the sky her mother has only one dream to see her daughter comfortably settled. Settlement for a girl usually means marriage. Sonali has her father as her ideal and he inculcates lofty ideals in her.

A bureaucrat herself, Sonali is working in a system which is rotten from its very roots. She has her own "fires and fevers of belief' (24). Sonali grows up with a dream to fulfil, "a new tradition to create (our) her independent worth to prove" (Sahgal 1987 : 24). When at Oxford Sonali is an idealist and holds dreamy views but when in India she enters bureaucracy, she realises how foolish she had been when she and Ravi were "...blissfully complacent, truly Victorian in their belief in India's inevitable progress, in peaceful change, in democracy everlasting" (98). She is the daughter of an able administrative officer with a broad vision. The father seems to have rubbed some of his ideals on his worthy daughter. Before her administrative services could entrust her with a responsibility, her father puts an important responsibility on her shoulder with the inspiring words : "Sonali, people like you, especially women like you, are going to Indianize India." (*Ibid.*)

Unlike other women Sonali strikes more as an individual than as a role model. And as such she faces more strident antagonists than those women who are fighting either as wives or as daughters. Sonali is fighting as an administrator against the whole system. She knows what is right and what is wrong. She can understand legal from illegal. She can smell a device and it is this ability precisely that brings her nemesis. When emergency is imposed she happens to understand what the real predicament was. This is her crime as she was supposed to pretend that, "The empress's new clothes were beautiful" (25). She knows :

> We know this was no emergency. If it had been, the priorities would have been quite different. We were all taking part in a thinly disguised masquerade, preparing the stage for family rule. And we were involved in a conspiracy of silence, which is why we were careful not to do more than say hello when we passed each other in the building, and not to talk about our work after hours which made after-hours sessions very silent indeed. No one wanted trouble (25).

Sonali, however, refuses to be a party to this silent sycophancy. As her father's daughter she decides to fight the oppressors with her indomitable will. Consequently she is "transferred without warning, demoted, punished and humiliated" (27). One could not, however, trace the origin of this strong will only in her upbringing because that is what Kiran — her sister — got as well. Kiran does not understand Sonali's stand, she weighs everything in terms of profit and loss. She does not see a crisis behind Sonali's transfer. Her simple suggestion is, "Well, then you could apologise and get reinstated or something" (32). Sonali, however, hates such worm-like existence. She is threatened by the "collective will to cowardice, when men and women in their millions, a whole nationful, did cowardly deeds?" (30)

It is not only at work place that Sonali shows such strong determination. As a young girl, she has kept all attempts to cow her into a bride at bay. She has seen only one example of a bride — that of Bimmie — which breeds repulsion and even horror in her mind, hence she refuses to catch the bait offered by her mother and Bhabi-jan. She observes :

> They were just waiting to catch me like flying fish are caught when they leap up out of the waves, like Bimmie had been caught in midair tossing a basketball into a net, waiting to say Ha! Got you! And turn you into a sweet and docile nature" (49).

As a girl she refused to be patted down into shape "as though she were an abnormally risen dough" (*ibid*). In fact this refusal to bow down is her first step to revolt and it shapes her future life. She does not want to get married before she has accomplished her dreams and the corollary to this is also true — she sets certain goals before herself, as she does not want to get married. She is initiated into a bright future by her father's advice. The refusal to wear contact lenses is symbolic of her conviction to live life on her own terms and her resolution that she shall not permit anyone to interfere with her affairs. In this she also anticipates Naomi Wolf's crusade against the 'beauty myth.'

Sonali has a sense of solidarity with women in general. Though herself not a common woman she has seen the pain of servility and with conscious efforts she has evaded its clutches; hence more than her Kachru like peers she esteems freedom and liberty highly. As a girl child in a patriarchal society, she finds people around her looking on her as valuable wife material. To her chagrin, even her mother joins these people who know only one way to appreciate the looks and talents of a girl — that of her viability in the marriage market. As a small child she didn't know the deeper significance of marriage, but she could sense efforts to cow her into a docile dumb doll and she could then feel an upsurge of antagonism against all such efforts. She was a libertine even before she could comprehend the meaning of liberty and she has a natural aversion to servility. Her mother wants her to pay visit to mataji — a self-proclaimed saint but Sonali, though a child had the guts to question the integrity of mataji — "what did she do to become a saint." Her convent background has made her familiar with saints who worked their way up to sainthood and earned their halos hence she could not accept a dumb saint. As an undergraduate student she has high ambitions and wants to go abroad in order to pursue higher studies. Her father has always been a spring of inspiration and it is from him that she learns self-assertiveness. She reminisces :

> And this is probably what drove me to frantic competition, to stardom in my studies, to deliberance from suitable 'boys' and marriage abroad. And to everything afterwards, from a career of my own to not wearing contact lenses and wanting my living room to look my own (51).

Marxism made its appearance as a powerful influence while she was still at Oxford. Along with her childhood friend Ravi she "...heard and responded to the siren song of Marxism" (98). But here again with her natural propensity to freedom and equality, Sonali takes Marxism more seriously and it gives her "trouble from the start" whereas for Ravi it is simply a "romance." For Ravi ideals matter only in books, he has never had a first-hand experience of the ugly, harsh facet of life, whereas being a woman, Sonali has seen it all and had fought the battle for survival in a man's world. She herself analyses this difference :

> I think he said that because he was a man. He had never fought a battle for freedom, never been patted down when his sap was rising, never had a sari throttling his legs, making walking in the wind and running to catch a bus a threat to life and limb, never had his mother set up a howl when he went and got a haircut. He had no idea what the simplest subjugation were all about. I, who did, had no intention of chaining myself to any doctrine when I had just lost some of my chains (101).

Though born in a male-dominated, parochial society, Sonali is not one of those women who not only meekly accept the shackles but also sometimes even take delight in them. She is influenced by her father who was a believer in woman's emancipation. She, like her creator Sahgal, belongs to a family where men had been strongly feminist. Going through her father's diary, she discovers herself. From her great grandfather's accounts she learns to present herself as a "person, not the personification of an image" (129). Her quest for identity takes new dimensions when she finds out her family seeds. She learns that her great grandfather had been a tremendously strong man and held highly liberal views even as back as 1915. In a discussion with one of the British officers, he defeated all his attempts to sidle away with the *sati* issue by saying : "It is not British territory" (122). He tells Mr. Timmons :

> But what was needed was a crusade with all its passion and fever. Generations of lawyers will uphold generations of laws but the old evils will go on into the twentieth and twenty-first centuries because no torch has been lit, and because you, who have the opportunity, don't seize the moment and break the back of evil when you have the chance (123-24).

These words serve as beacon light for Sonali. It is as if she gets the answer to her Hamlet like dilemma — to do or not to do. She decides to fight her crusade. The diary makes a compelling impact on her. She observes : "I saw a world revealed. And I fell asleep to dreams of heroisms, whose company I was scarcely fit to keep" (*ibid.*). She resolves that if there has to be someone to light the torch first, it has to be herself. Further, the story of her courageous great grandmother who fought her greedy relatives after her husband's death, fills her with inspiration. Despite all her fortitude her great grandmother was burnt alive by her relatives who then spread stories that she had performed *sati.* Sonali learns that she is not alone in her fight for rights, there have been many others before her. She realises : "Not all of us are passive before cruelty and depravity" (136).

Sonali is a woman in a man's world. Challenging all norms of the male-dominated society and establishing her own standards, she keeps up her fight against evil as she is confident that in the bargain she has "nothing to lose but her chains" (98). She dares to make her own world where there are no predators, there is love, there is faith, there is Rose and there is her father as a soothing, inspiring influence. Here is a woman who is truly free inasmuch as she is not ready to sacrifice her ideals even for the sake of her love — Ravi Kachru. On this issue she does not compromise and prefers the life of a spinster than that of a second fiddle that an average Indian wife is. To her soul-mate, her confidante Rose, she bares her bosom : "...but he is so rigid, so bossy, so selfish, if I married him I'd have to agree with him all the time" (180). This is why she had not contemplated marriage. In her refusal to marry Ravi, Sonali shines like tomorrow's woman.

Ravi and Sonali are somewhere deep down kindred souls. The difference between them is the difference between their circumstances. Sonali has been moulded by a strong father whereas Ravi has been weighed down by Bhabi-jan's practical approach. A true iconoclast, she breaks the myth of 'woman for hearth and men for sword.' While Ravi breaks down before oppression Sonali defies all attempts to crush her individuality even at the cost of her career. She is not one to breakdown, instead she is moved with indignation against all injustice. It is not only for herself that she fights but also for others. The wrong treatment meted out to Rose by her stepson Dev enrages her and she requests Ravi to use his influence over the former in order to make matters smooth. The cold blooded murder of Rose leaves her seething with anger :

> Far from finding formal words of condolence or squeezing so much as a single tear out of my dry unslept eyes, I felt a freezing, baffling anger I couldn't explain (221).

This is how she reacts to injustice — not as a so-called ideal woman is supposed to do but as a crusader. This trait of Sonali disappoints her flirtatious male colleagues and they feel she has 'a man's mind' (153). Dev's callous trcatment of Rose angers her as much as the plight of the beggar who has lost her arms to tyrants. Fighting for justice comes to her naturally and as such she does not understand passivity against oppression. She enlightens the beggar about his legal rights :

> There are laws to protect tenants. Didn't you put your sharecropping arrangements on land record? Wasn't there some evidence of it? (227)

It is this inner strength that brings her close to the millennium woman. It is this moral courage that makes even her rivals realise her worth. Ravi Kachru — her friend turned rival who had shared some of her idealism salutes her convictions. Sonali and Ravi together had visualised dreams and Marxism had together influenced them but somewhere down the line they got estranged as Ravi developed a pragmatic approach to life. While Sonali sticks to her ideals and is prepared to face all consequences without any grudges, Ravi breaks even as he faces slightest opposition. For Ravi survival is more important, hence he compromises but for Sonali moral triumph is more important than trivial victory in her career. It is because of her spirit that Ravi comes round to her views and says : "You were too brave for me. You set impossible standards" (230) and also he does not forget to add : "It's too late now, but if we had our time over again, I'd work it out differently" (*ibid.*). It is here that Sonali shines as the millennium woman. Herein shines her strength and her conviction. While she has no remorse for losing her job, Ravi is reproachful for his losing his ideals. Sonali confesses to Ravi that she had been in love with him but she could never bring herself to compromise on her principles. Thus Sonali is saved from falling in love instead she rises as she opens the eyes of her man. Such recent creations as Virmati in *Difficult Daughters* pale before her. While Sonali controls her emotions and refuses to marry Ravi, Virmati marries the professor who is already married and accepts the life of shameful surveillance.

Sonali deserves the crown of the millennium woman because despite all odds she does not lose faith. A victim of the pervert system, she had to resign when she refused to compromise, yet she does not lose hope nor does she contemplate leaving her country. With an inherent confidence she decides to start her career afresh with Marcella and Brian. This she does without any ill will or remorse : "I was young and alive, with my own century stretched out before me, waiting to be lived" (234).

Sonali has all the traits of the millennium woman. She is the woman of future — intelligent, witty, strong, confident, courageous and enterprising. Though conceived in the eighties she outshines most of her recent counterparts inasmuch as she stands on her own without using a man as her crutches. Steeped in the values of her father who taught her the ideals of non-violence, she somehow comes to realise the futility of non-violence as a mode of protest against dictators : "If all the mice in the world stopped running away and stood their ground, cats would stop killing them" (127). It is this faith that serves as *mantra* or the guiding force of her life. She resembles Ellen Goodman's 'Anonyma' who she describes as :

> "But my Anonyma is more than the sum total of the unknown female creators of the millennium. She also represents the forgotten mass of women who took part in all the movements that literally moved women forward." (http://boulderdailycamera.com)

WORKS CITED

Sahgal, Nayantara, *A Time to be Happy.* New Delhi : Sterling, 1958.

——, *This Time of Morning.* New Delhi : Orient Paperbacks, 1965.

——, *The Day in Shadow.* Calcutta : Penguin Books, 1971.

——, *Rich Like Us.* London : Heinemann, 1985.

Wolf, Naomi, *The Beauty Myth.* New York : William Morrow, 1991, p. 12 : She describes the beauty myth that is more disastrous than even the feminine mystique which Betty Friedan talked about. Wolf writes : "It is no accident that so many potentially powerful women feel this way. We are in the midst of a violent backlash against feminism that uses images of female beauty as a weapon against women's advancement : the beauty myth."

10

Marital Disharmony in Anita Desai's Novels

—*Basavaraj Naikar*

OF ALL the contemporary Indian English novelists Anita Desai is, perhaps, the most perceptive and consistent explorer of the inner life, especially that of Indian women, convulsed by an acute sense of helplessness in the face of the onslaughts of an unfeeling world and the resultant mental agony. Even in her very first novel, *Cry, The Peacock,* she attempts to inscape the turbulent inner world of its protagonist, Maya, whose neurotic condition is brought about by a variety of factors including marital discord and barrenness and psychic disorder. Using a tripartite structure and third person narration, which affords opportunities for authorial comment, Anita Desai traces Maya's gradual descent into a state of madness, impelled by her responses to the developments in her outer life, as it were.

Married at an early age to Gautama, a friend of her father and leading lawyer, who is of twice her age Maya seems destined to suffer from emotional starvation especially since she is childless. The first emotional crisis she faces arises at the death of her pet dog, Toto, on whom she has been lavishing all her affection. The opening chapter detailing it reports how Maya first could not stand the sight of her beloved dead dog and that she rushes to "the garden tap to wash the vision from her eyes" (p. 5). Maya thinks that "she saw the evil glint of a blue bottle" (p. 5) and grows hysterical and finds the setting sun "swelling visibly like...a purulent boil" (p. 6). Her condition is aggravated by Gautama's causal and unfeeling remarks : "It is all over, come and drink your tea and stop crying. You mustn't cry" (p. 7). Further, instead of consoling her in her grief at the loss of her Toto, he leaves her to meet a visitor who has come to see him and forgets all about the dead dog. This incident brings out the contrast between Maya, who is highly sensitive and imaginative and of a neurotic sensibility, and Gautama, who is unimaginative and pragmatic and unsentimental — a contrast accentuated by communication gap on account of his being wrapped up in his professional preoccupations. It is, therefore, not surprising that there have been constantly quarreling with each other even over trifles. Maya, reflecting on her unhappy marriage, observes :

> It was discouraging to reflect on how much in her marriage was based upon a nobility forced upon us from outside, and therefore neither true nor lasting. It was broken repeatedly, and repeatedly the pieces were picked up and put together again, as of a sacred icon with which out of the pettiest superstition, we could not bear to part (p. 45).

Although, they continue to live together, they find their temperaments irreconcilable and their sensibilities marked by divergence. Surprised by Gautama's inability to differentiate between the smell of lemons and petunias Maya muses :

> The blossoms of the lemon tree were different, quite different; of much stronger, crisper character, they seemed cut out of hard moon shells, by a sharp knife of mother of pearl, into curving, scimitar petals that guarded the heart of fragrance. Their scent, too, was more vivid — a sour, astringent scent, refreshing as that of ground lemon peel, a crushed lemon leaf. I tried to explain this to Gautama, stammering with anxiety, for now, when his companionship was a necessity, I required his closest understanding (p. 21).

It is not merely Gautama's insensitivity as is implied in his inability to distinguish between the two smells but his being inured to the beauty of the natural world and unresponsive to her feelings traceable in part to his philosophical detachment that makes for their estrangement. Maya feels sorry for her husband :

> ...Poor Gautama. Not to be able to notice the odour of limes, not to hear the melancholy voice singing somewhere behind the plantains, not to have time to count the stars as they came out one by one — poor Gautama, my poor, poor husband... (p. 237).

Indeed, she feels that Gautama "had never lived, and never would" (p. 240). The temperamental incompatibility that characterises their relationship brings about an unbridgeable gulf between them causing acute mental agony to the highly strung Maya whose condition is aggravated by her father-fixation, as observed by the perceptive though unresponsive Gautama, when she harks back to her childhood memories to avoid the present :

> If you know your Freud, it would be very straight-forward...you have a very obvious father-obsession which is also the reason why you married me, a man so much older than yourself. It is a complex that, unless you mature rapidly, you will not be able to deal with, to destroy. But then, it will probably destroy itself in the end, since passion of this sort is almost always self-consuming, having no object within its range that it can safely consume. Any little setback destroys it...(pp. 168-69).

Indeed, it is her 'father-obsession' which has made her marry Gautama, so much older than herself and friend of her father and which accounts for her turning to childhood memories and lapsing into childhood behaviour as evidenced by her crying and bursting out into a fit of furious pillow-beating to seek release from the oppressive present. Maya even remarks : "The world is like a toy specially made for me, painted in my favourite colours, set moving to my favourite tunes" (p. 41).

Further, her neurotic condition has worsened by her recollection of a prediction by an albino astrologer in her childhood :

> My child, I would not speak of it if I saw it on your face alone. But look, look at the horoscope. Stars do not lie. And it is best to warn you, prepare you.... Death to one of you. When you are married — and you shall be married young.... Death — an early one — by unnatural causes (p. 33).

Obsessed with the albino astrologer's ominous preddiction, Maya muses :

> It must be a mark on my forehead, which had been so clear to the opaque eye of the albino who had detected it, upon which the stars now hurled themselves vengefully, and which prophesied a relentless and fatal competition between myself and Gautama. I tried to define the mark, give it a name, a locality. Was it an arrow? A coffin? A star? Was it between the eyes? At the temple? Was it dark? Was it pale? And what made the gods reach out and touch it with their cold fingers, as they considered the prospect of a murder? (p. 122)

Further, she is aware of her being confined to her private hell : "Torture, guilt, dread, imprisonment — these were the four walls of my private hell, one that no one could survive in long. Death was certain" (p. 117). Her obsession with death reinforced by the death of her pet dog plunges her into a state of insanity of which she is uncannily conscious as she herself observes :

> Yes, I am going insane. I am moving further and further from all wisdom, all calm, and I shall soon be mad, if I am not that already. Perhaps it is my madness that leads me to imagine that horoscope, that encounter with the albino, his prediction, my fate? Perhaps it is only a phenomenon of insanity? (p. 124)

Maya is convinced that she is becoming insane as she herself remarks :

> This is not natural, I told myself, this cannot be natural. There is something weird about me now, wherever I go, whatever I see, whatever I listen to has this unnaturalness to it. This is insanity. But who, what is insane? I myself? Or the world around me? (p. 167)

In her insane condition she becomes all the more obsessed with death, which makes her think that "it was now to be either Gautama, or I." Faced with such a terrible choice she decides that Gautama has to die as he is detached from and indifferent to what makes life livable.

It is significant that even before becoming insane she contemplates murder as is brought out by her remark that murders are committed "only for the sake of money, or property — or anything solid, and dirty. Not for love, or life or basic things" (p. 23). That she should think of it at all suggests her longing for a life of freedom possible only through the death of Gautama, which later becomes accentuated when she receives a letter from her brother, Arjun, informing her of his having 'rebelled' against their father and the socio-cultural tradition that have inhibited the development of his individuality. Ironically enough, her yearning for freedom seems fulfilled by her insanity which drives her to murder her husband. What is 'heard' at the end of the novel is not the shriek which a gruesome murder would cause but "the patter of a child's laughter cascading up and down the scales of some new delight — a brilliant peacock feather perhaps?" (p. 251) followed by silence as she commits suicide which represents her release from the grasping world. The novel traces the disintegration of Maya as her overwrought mind plunges her into darkness of death.

Anita Desai's fourth novel, *Where Shall We Go This Summer* (1975) like her first novel, *Cry, The Peacock,* focuses on marital disharmony which accentuated the emotionally highly strong nature of their protagonists, Sita and Maya, respectively. In some respects, *Where Shall We Go This Summer* ? is reminiscent of D.H. Lawrence's story, "The Woman Who Rode Away," although the comparison between the two cannot be sustained as they sharply differ in their essential thematic concerns. However, like the heroine of Lawrence's tale, Sita, the protagonist of Desai's novel, faced with an unwanted fifth pregnancy goes away from Bombay along with her two children, Menaka and Karan, leaving behind her husband, Raman, in despair. Sita after her marriage finds living in her husband's parents' house, "their age-rotted flat, "unbearable in that it is marked by "sub-human placidity, calmness and sluggishness" and feels that "their subhumanity might swamp her." To preserve her individuality, she behaves in a way, which appears to be outrageous to the other members of the family by smoking openly and talking "in sudden rushes of emotion, as though flinging darts at their smooth, unscared faces." Indeed, she regards most of the people as animals : "They are nothing — nothing but appetite and sex. Only food, sex and money matter — Animals" (pp. 31-32). She compares them to pariahs :

> My pet animals — or wild animals in the forest, yes. But these are neither — They are like pariahs you see in the street, hanging about the drains and dustbins, waiting to pounce and kill and eat (p. 32).

Later, she shifts to a small flat with her husband and children but does not find life any better as she has to endure visits by people whose "insularity and complacence" (p. 33) "as well as the aggression and violence of others" (p. 33) act as "affronts upon her tiring nerves" (p. 33). Further, Sita becomes increasingly alienated from the world as she is paid little attention to by her husband because of his being absorbed in the management of his business and her children because of their growing independent with the result that she is faced with intolerable boredom that can prove destructive :

> She herself looking in it saw it, stretched out so vast, so flat, so deep, that in fright she scrambled about it, searching for a few of those moments that proclaimed her still alive, not quite drowned and dead (pp. 33-34).

Indeed, Sita has had to suffer boredom and loneliness to which modern man seems sentenced and her plight is reminiscent of that of Antoine Roquentin's in Jean Paul Sartre's *Nausea,* who is tormented by his traceable to ennui and alienation. Though bearing the legendary names, Sita and her husband Rama, they spell a relationship, which is a travesty of that immortalised by the characters concerned in *Ramayana.* Sita being highly imaginative and emotional and Raman being 'a middling kind of man,' prosaic and phlegmatic, they are temperamentally poles apart which accounts for their being unable to forge a harmonious marital relationship. For instance, recalling a month later, their encounter with a stranger on their way back home from their visit to Ajanta and Ellora :

> "He seemed so brave," she blurted when Raman asked her why she had once more brought up the subject of hitch-hiking foreigner, months later. "Brave? Him?" Raman was honestly amused, "he was a fool — he didn't even know which side of the road to wait on."
>
> "Perhaps that was only innocence," Sita faltered, "and it made him seem more brave not knowing anything but going on nevertheless" (p. 34).

Sita's comment which must have seemed absurd or irrational to her husband highlights the psychological distance separating them as also their sharply differing perceptions traceable to her yearning for a life of freedom and his matter-of-fact attitude to life respectively. Her anguish has become unbearable when she finds herself pregnant once again — for the fifth time and deciding to have 'a bewitched life' for herself and her unborn child, she leaves for Manori, a small island off the Marve island, where her father has built a house, hoping to "achieve the miracle of not giving birth," taking her two children, Menaka and Karan, with her. Moses, the caretaker of the house, escorts them across the sea to her father's island house which being unoccupied for twenty years is in a sorry state :

> ...then she went in at last and saw what had become of the house in twenty years of absence — a waste of ashes she saw, the cold remains of the bonfire her father had lit to a blaze...the odour was of bate and mildew; and silence boomed like the silence of undersea caves. It had no air of providing shelter from the sea or beach — it was much a natural part of them as an abandoned shell or lump of twisted drift-wood (p. 18).

After unpacking her things and lying down with her children, Sita ruminates recalling her unhappy married life and her childhood spent on the island with her father who had become a legend in his lifetime having brought water from the well to the inhabitants of the island and taught them more profitable ways of farming, although she was sceptical about his being a messiah as she found his relationship with her own elder sister, Rekha, who later on became a national celebrity, rather incestuous. Indeed, recollecting her father, she wonders whether her father was really a true saint and patriot and what had made his second wife desert him and her children and live a life of seclusion secretly in Varanasi and significantly, she is not able to find answers to those questions which remain unanswered in the novel. Interestingly, while her father plays a Prospero-like role in Manori as in Shakespeare's *Temptest,* Sita does not behave like Miranda although she views "the island as a piece of magic, a magic mirror."

Her reverie-like reminiscing, presented as a stream of consciousness, is reminiscent of Mrs. Ramsay's in Virginia Woolf's *To the Lighthouse* in that it underlines the tension between the materialist male world and the female world marked by sensitivity, although the comparison between the two novels cannot be pressed far beyond the fact that both exemplify in different ways "fiction of intensified sensitivity." Significantly, Sita's daughter, Menaka, does not share her mother's poetic or artistic temperament or perception as is evidenced by an argument she has with her. Sita discussing the poverty of science and the opulence of art observes : "Science don't be as satisfactory. It is all — all figures, statistics, logic. Science is believing that two and two make four — pooh" (p. 85) and adds "It leads you to a dead-end. There are no dead-ends, now, in art. That is something spontaneous, Menaka, and alive and creative" (p. 85). Menaka brushes aside her argument terming it "all nonsense."

Sita's attempt to overcome her existential despair stemming from her alienation from her husband and her children, who long for the comforts and excitement of city life, proves abortive. Menaka writes to her father asking him to take them back as she has to apply for admission to the Medical College. Seeing how excited her children at the time of her husband's arrival, Sita feels "that they were being disloyal to her, disloyal to the island and its wild nature" (p. 94). Raman's arrival and the conversation that she has with him have the effect of confronting her with the stark actualities of life, which cannot be wished away. She realises, though painfully, like the heroine of R.K. Narayan's *The Dark Room,* that there is no escape from one's responsibilities and that life must be continued :

> ...Life must be continued, and all its business — Menaka's admission to medical college gained, wife led to hospital, now child safely brought forth, the children reared, the factory seen to, a salary earned, a salary spent...(p. 101).

She even felt herself to be an escapist and coward :

> She had escaped from duties and responsibilities, from order and routine, from life and the city, to unlivable island. She had refused to give birth to a child in a world not fit to receive the child. She had the imagination to offer it an alternative — a life unlived, a life bewitched. She had cried out her grand "No" but now the time had come for her epitaph to be written — *che fece per viltate il gron refiute.* Very soon now that epitaph would have to be written (p. 102).

Just as R.K. Narayan's heroine returns home after quitting it like Nora of Ibsen's *The Doll's House,* Sita picks up her belongings and prepares to leave the island with her husband and children, feeling "like a player at the end of the performance, clearing the stage, packing the costumes, in equal parts saddened and relieved." She regards her sojourn on the island as an episode in a drama — the drama of existence, in her case :

> ...Her time on the island had been very much of an episode on a stage, illuminated by gaudy sunset effects and played to thunderous storm's music, the storm ended, the play over, the stage had now to be cleared — then the player could go home. Instead of being a person who for many years had had to perform on a false stage and had only her, on the island, begun to live a life of primitive reality, she had actually been playing the part here of an

> actress in a theatrical performance and was now to return to a life of retirement, off stage (pp. 110-11).

Sita's frustration is traceable to her futile attempt to relive her past as she did in her childhood forgetting that the passage of time inexorably alters everything including herself, which explains why she finds the islanders unresponsive and critical of her, comparing her with her father. Further, she is made to admit to herself "that destruction may be the true element in which life survives and creation merely a freak, temporary, and doomed event" (pp. 37-38) as she battles to save her unborn child from the violence-ridden world. Significantly, she becomes aware of it when she helplessly watches her children acting violently :

> Karan kicked over a tower of blocks and howled with maniac glee to see them tumble; Menaka sat calmly tearing her Sunday water colours into long strips of meaningless colour, her husband casually handed her the newspaper on his way out to the office. They all hammered at her with cruel fists.... They were hand-grenades all hurled at her frail gold fish-bowl belly and instinctively she laid her hands over it, feeling the child there play like some soft fleshed fish in a bowl of warm sea-water. She folded her hands over it, frightened, certain now that civilization had been created by the god-like efforts of the few, in the face of timeless war of destruction that had begun with time and was now roaring around her, battering her and her fish-foetus so that survival seemed hopeless. How could civilization survive, how could the child? How could she hold them whole and pure and unimpeached in the midst of this bloodshed? They would surely be wounded, fall and die (p. 37).

The island to which she goes in the hope that it will provide a sanctuary for her tortured self seems as suffocating as the city, confronting her with a kind of primitive reality that proves as unbearable as the dreary reality that her home in the city spells to which she has to be reconciled if she is to commit herself in life and motherhood.

Where Shall We Go This Summer may thus be seen as a parable on the inability of human beings to relate the inner with the outer, the individual with society. It is a story of illusions melting away in the cold light of the everyday and the commonplace. It does suggest that a life of complete inwardness is not the solution to the problems of life. Nor is the other extreme of complete conformity and total draining out of the individuality and of the imagination of the human being the proper way out of the dilemma. It shows that human happiness consists in harmonising the opposites of life.

WORKS CITED

Anita Desai, *Cry, The Peacock.* Calcutta : Rupa and Co., 1980. All the further references to the text are to this edition only.

Anita Desai, *Where Shall We Go This Summer.* Delhi : Vikas Publishing House, 1975. All the further references to the text are to this edition only.

11

Discovery of the Self : An Interior Journey in Margaret Atwood's *Surfacing* and Anita Desai's *Where Shall We Go This Summer?*

—S.N. Vikram Raj Urs

IN THIS paper an attempt is made to focus on the basic quest of a solitary individual as dramatized in Margaret Atwood's *Surfacing* and Anita Desai's *Where Shall We Go This Summer*? These novelists hailing from totally different cultural contexts take up the interior journey of a human being, an archetypal figure who struggles for a new pattern of order. Their protagonists try to rediscover a creative possibility within the invisible layers of their self. The woman, in these two novels, is the archetypal figure who tries to find her moorings to extricate herself from her anguished state. There are striking similarities in the respective approaches of Anita Desai and Margaret Atwood. They share a similar belief in concentrating on the submerged inner world of an individual.

Anita Desai explains in a key passage that, 'writing is to me a process of discovering truth — the truth that is nine-tenth's of the iceberg that is submerged beneath the one-tenth visible portion we call Reality. Writing is my way of plunging to the depths and exploring the underlying truth.'

A study of the fiction of Anita Desai reveals the creative potentialities of a human being who is cramped in by her associations with social mores and conventions which reflect her connections with the objective world. Maya (*Cry, the Peacock*), Sita (*Where Shall We Go This Summer*?), and Bim (*Clear Light of Day*) explore a definite meaning for their existence. Maya searches 'for an order of lines and designs, a symmetry' in order to discover solace for her inner rage. Sita travels back to her past to find out a meaning to her present life. Similarly, Margaret Atwood's *Edible Woman* and *Surfacing* in particular deal with the theme of confronting the submerged layers of the self. The outer skin of an individual is peeled off and the essential core is in perfect union with the cosmos. *Surfacing* is an archetypal search of a nameless narrator to find out the creative sources of life. This search for a new being is fully probed in *Surfacing* and *Where Shall We Go This Summer?*

Where Shall We Go This Summer? deals with the story of a young disillusioned woman, Sita. She wishes to go back to her childhood past, her parental house, Manori. The island of Manori is cut off from the mainland. She also wishes to cut herself off from the mainland, Bombay. It is her desire to go to the island and live where her father was a respected figure. He was a Gandhian who has left his unmistakable stamp on the island. She desperately tries to recapture her childhood days when she was happy and secure in the company of her father.

The starting point of plunging into the invisible mysterious past is that she decides to go back to the island. The island is a romantic metaphor for Sita who values the heroic and redeeming qualities of her father. But when she travels back to the island which is almost deserted, she painfully reconstructs her submerged past. She discovers that her father is not a true Gandhian at heart. She also realizes that the sea is dangerous and evil. It is not the sea which represented her childhood memories. The very name Sita reminds us of the suffering qualities of the exiled Sita in *The Ramayana.* This Sita is an extension of the archetypal figure of Sita. She makes a deliberate choice and she is exiled from her disillusionment with her husband and from false social values.

There is an attempt to understand personal relationships through the character of Sita. An intimate rapport with Raman her husband is possible only if Sita tries to re-adjust her inner realities to the outside 'meaningless' world. The novel develops from the germinating idea that it would be impossible to go on living in a state of inner contradictions. A sensitive individual will have to make a sacrifice of giving a part of oneself to make way for a meaningful personal relationship.

Sita has an answer to her dilemma in Cavafy's poem. She quotes from the poem and it consoles her to a great extent. The poem reappears in the final section of the novel. She is not sure whether to say the 'great Yes' or the 'great No'. The essence of the poem is that an individual who has the courage to say 'the right No' is absolutely 'free' from life's 'dull-lit empty shell.'

The innermost urge of Sita is to identify herself with 'the right No.' She almost says 'the right No' to the 'order and routine' life with Raman. But she is not fully prepared to go to that extent of defying the ordinariness of her existence. She meekly submits to Raman's wish to take her back to the mainland. But she is determined to wage a ceasless 'battle between his brand of courage and hers.'

On the surface, Margaret Atwood's *Surfacing,* recounts the experiences of a young Canadian divorcee who returns to her home of the childhood with three friends. She fails as a painter and her name is not mentioned. Her lover Joe accompanies her. He is a potter who does not make the grade. Her other two friends, David, a failed rebel and Anna, a failed wife also go with her in search of her 'lost' father. The nameless narrator wants to investigate the sudden disappearance of her father from an isolated island in one of the large lakes of Northern Quebec.

When she returns to the island she is exposed to memories of her childhood. The wild island exerts its elemental hold on the consciousness of the nameless narrator. The search for her father leads onto something else — an exploration of her inner self, her nature as a woman and her place in Nature. She is submerged into a mystical vision when she dives into the lake from which she surfaces to re-discover her lost innocence, with a new acceptance of herself and her spiritual powers in the natural world.

Like Sita, the nameless narrator rejects her oppressive environment. She rebels against the false materialism and vulgarity of the American society. She rejects her marriage. She distrusts love as a form of male possessiveness. Sita too does not want love to be an aspect of male domination. The nameless narrator is a divorcee with a sense of guilt. The dead body of the child under water brings on a sudden memory that she had an abortion. She travels back to the lonely island disgusted with the false notions of floating on the surface life. Similar to the agitated self of Sita who is fed up with the ugly life of Bombay, the nameless narrator has a strong desire to find out an order, a balance to her inner fury on the island. She tries to explore the rock paintings beneath the lake. She wants to understand the secret language. She plunges into the lake and many realizations occur to her. In the process of knowing her past, she is transformed into a new being.

The novel is a continuation, a renewal of life in the self of the nameless narrator. Her dive into the lake below the surface is a crucial event : she is descending into her subconscious. She has recognized her dead father. It is also a nightmare of her lost child. She dies a symbolic death beneath the surface :

> 'I couldn't accept it, that mutilation, ruin I'd made, I needed a different version.'

She is separated into two parts, owing to the raging conflict within. One part exists on the visible world. Another part is buried under the surface. Her relationships with her ex-husband, her present lover Joe and David and Anna, her friends who are known to her very recently consist of one separate self. The direct encounter of her father's corpse leads onto the surfacing from death into renewal of life. She identifies through the dive into her invisible part, her 'free-floating' new born self. She realizes her twin-double :

> "My other shape was in the water,
> not my reflection but my shadow,
> foreshortened, outline blurred,
> rays streaming out from around the head" (p. 141)

The re-living of the memories of her past is a process in her psychic quest.

She is able to capture lucid moments of pristine spiritual harmony with Nature through the re-enactment of her memory and by observing her relationship with her friends David and Ann and her lover Joe. She emerges as a 'whole' woman cured of her sick disease of the mind :

> "When I am clean I come up out of the lake,
> leaving my false body floated on the surface,
> a cloth decoy; it jiggles in the waves I make,
> nudges, gently against the dock.
> They offered clothing as a token, formerly;
> that was partial but the gods are demanding,
> absolute, they want all." (p. 178)

She joins herself into the mysterious, elemental forces of Nature. She is in a mystical travel. '...accepts me as part of the land' and 'Around me the space rustles; owl sound, across the lake or inside me, distance contracts. A light wind, the small waves talking against the shore, multilingual water are indications of the change that has happened.'

She sheds all she has acquired from society and lives alone. She lives like a wild beast on roots. She returns to a consciousness beyond her rational self. She hopes that her unborn child will be 'the first true human.' She has a vision of her father in which he realizes that he is an intruder upon Nature. The father makes a determined effort to destroy his cabin. The rational mind gives way to a heightened state. It is possible for a secret communion with the dark powers of Nature. Her return to 'my own time' will be based on new energies which are released from a life-enhancing 'power.'

The important difference lies in the fact that in *Where Shall We Go This Summer*? Sita goes to the mainland still clinging to keep her individual freedom secretly. But in *Surfacing,* the Nameless narrator fully evolves into a new being who is free of guilt and shame. She merges with the living preserves of Nature. The dive into the lake and the surfacing point to a state of 'To Trust is to let go.'

WORKS CITED

Anita Desai, *Where Shall We Go This Summer?* Vikas Publishing House, Delhi, 1975, Orient Paperbacks, Delhi, 1982.

Margaret Atwood, *Surfacing,* Virago, London, 1972. Rpt. 1983.

12

Frailty Thy Name is Woman : A Feminist Perspective of Anita Desai's *Fasting, Feasting**

—Asha Choubey

IN THE days of Adam and Eve, inequality of sexes was not known but down the ages women have been relegated to an inferior position in the social set-up. From being the very incarnation of Power (Shakti) and Knowledge (Gnyan), women came to be held only as a child-bearing machine and their horizons have been supposed to be confined only to their familial role. Chiefly the blame was put on men and it was believed that male-domination does not allow women to flourish freely. But in recent times there have also been sensitive writers who have taken a humanist approach to the situation. They have taken a holistic view of the issue and have discovered that it's not only male-chauvinism that has caused havoc but also female-reluctance to face the challenges and even female-apathy that is responsible for this disparity. In the last couple of years *Difficult Daughters* by Manju Kapoor and *Fasting, Feasting* by Anita Desai are two attempts to take stock of the situation from this viewpoint. Primarily the story of human hungers, *Fasting, Feasting* merits appreciation from a feminist point of view. Like all women writers, Desai is not only sensitive to women-question but also all 'criticism of life' from her pen can be finally seen

* This paper is a modified form of the paper presented at the V annual conference of Indian Association for Studies in Contemporary Literature at Bareilly College, Bareilly on 29-30 December, 1999.

as gynocriticism (Showalter 1989 : 4). This paper is an attempt to present a feminist approach to *Fasting, Feasting.* The novel, divided neatly into two parts, takes us to the centre of an extremely orthodox Indian family on one hand, and an unusually whimsical family in Massachusetts on the other. Apart from the head MamaPapa, Uma, Aruna and Arun form the Indian family whereas the family in Massachusetts consists of Mr. and Mrs. Patton, Rod and Melanie. Arun forms the link between these two families, which are socially, nationally and culturally different. Desai simply point out the emotional and human affinity that makes the two families one.

I

Primarily *Fasting, Feasting* is the story of Uma, who happens to be the most subdued — rather crushed member of the Indian family. Uma is like a catalyst whose presence is never noticed, never appreciated and yet whose absence may make all the difference. Uma is a woman lost in the jungle of duties — sometimes to her MamaPapa, at other times to her brother Arun and at still other times to her sister Aruna. She is expected to be an obedient daughter, an affectionate and motherly sister and everything but an individual. As a young girl, Uma has her dreams, her desires, but when her dreams come in conflict with the comforts of her parents it is she who has to sacrifice and she does. At the outset itself the novelist presents the contrast that exists between the colourful, happy life of her parents and her own dull and deary existence :

> Uma flounces off, her grey hair frazzled, her myopic eyes glaring behind her spectacles, muttering under her breath. The parents, momentarily agitated upon their swing by the sudden invasion of ideas — sweets, parcel, letter, sweets — settle back to their slow, rhythmic swinging. (Desai 1999 : 5)

The Atharva Veda says : The birth of a girl, grant it elsewhere, here grant a boy. (vi, 23)

If this could be the prayer of an age when the condition of women was relatively better and they were granted an almost equal status in the society, we may very well imagine the poor lot of women in other ages. Even educated parents show their primitive, rustic face today when it comes to choosing between daughter and son. Girls are not only less preferred but also they are more burdened with responsibilities. Women are expected to take care of their siblings. A woman is never allowed to be a child, right from her childhood she is supposed to act as a mother to her younger brothers and sisters. Since the birth of her baby brother Arun, Uma has been trained to sacrifice her private pleasures at the altar of familial responsibilities. Much like Virmati of *Difficult Daughters,* Uma is forced to nurse her kid brother, even when she is herself a child :

> When Mama came home, weak, exhausted and short-tempered, she tried to teach Uma the correct way of folding nappies, of preparing watered milk, of rocking the screaming infant to sleep when he was covered with prickly heat as with a burn. Uma, unfortunately, was her clumsy, undependable self, dropping and breaking things, frightenedly pulling away from her much too small, too precious and too fragile brother. (17-18)

Desai brings into focus parental apathy which scars the daughters permanently. First it is parents craving for a boy that hurts the daughters because it makes obvious the truth of their accidental birth. Had the parents been given a choice they would never have liked to face the ignominy of giving birth to a female child. Then it is their ecstasy at the birth of a son that makes the wounds even deeper, beyond cure. Papa celebrates the birth of Arun as he had never done the birth of Uma and Aruna.

> Papa, in his elation leaping over three chairs in the hall, one after the other, like a boy playing leap-frog, his arms flung up in the air and his hair flying. 'A boy!' he screamed a bo-oy! Arun, Arun at last!' (17)

Feminists maintain that women are not mentally different since birth. The female-child is only biologically different but the parochial society conditions it into being a woman :

> One is not born but rather becomes a woman, says Simone de Beauvoir. She continues, "No biological,

> psychological, economic fate determines the figure that the human female presents in the society, it is civilisation as a whole that produces this creature, intermediate between male and eunuch, which is described as feminine." (Beauvoir 1957 : 445)

Uma becomes a victim to the tendency of society to condition a girl-child to submit to the norms of the patriarchal set-up. Desai as a true humanist puts the blame not only on men who are suffering with the complex of male-superiority but also on women who oppress their own kind. It is not only the male-chauvinist that acts as the antagonist force but also apathetic female does more harm in terms of the loss of woman-soul. Uma is reduced to the status of a domestic help. All this because her mother has to fulfil her role of, 'Papa's helpmeet, his consort' as 'After all Uma and Aruna and the ayah were there to stand in for her at Arun's cot' (31). No efforts to cow down the already docile spirit of Uma are spared. She is denied the pleasure of ordinary living. If she once enjoys a cheerful evening out with Ramu Bhai, she has to bear her mother's curse : 'Quiet, you hussy! Not another word from you, you idiot child!'.... 'You, you disgrace to the family — nothing but disgrace, ever!' (53)

'Marriage is the destiny traditionally offered to women by society,' say the feminists (De Beauvoir : 445). Twice MamaPapa try to get Uma married, and twice it is that she is put to much humiliation and disgrace. When both the attempts end in fiasco, it is accepted that Uma has to remain unwed all her life and with a heavy heart her parents accept this burden. Though she never rebels, never utters a word of complaint, she is certainly not an unfeeling brute. She suffers silently, and solace does not come even from the most expected quarters — her mother. To make the matters worse Mama also looks upon her as an object of laughter.

Uma's sister Aruna is married off into a respectable family and moves to Bombay. Her brother Arun goes to Massachusetts to pursue higher education but Uma is left behind to serve her parents untiringly, to become the object of their barbs and to live a life of desolation. In this apathetic, friendless world Uma finds refuge in her childhood memories when she was still studying in school. Those were the golden days of her life, never again in her life she gets to taste such bliss as she had experienced then. Whenever she finds her present aimless existence too dreary to tolerate, she escapes into that world again. She has carefully preserved the Christmas cards and snapshots belonging to that period and the very sight and touch of these thrill her with ecstasy :

> She runs her finger along the gilt crosses and embossed poinsettias, she plays with fragments of ribbon and lace, and reads through the merry little jingles that make her smile : they are so loving and bright with goodwill and friendship, she binds them all up again with string and stows them away like treasure — to her they are treasure. If anyone were to touch, their magic would be somehow defaced : that is how she feels about them. (98-99)

Mama herself has no time for her family and home because she is always busy attending kitty parties and club meetings but when Mrs. O'Henry invites Uma to a coffee party, much hue and cry is raised. Even a single phone call invites the wrath of Papa :

> 'Costs money! Costs money!' he kept shouting long after. 'Never earned anything in her life, made me spend and spend, on her dowry and her wedding. Oh, yes, spend till I'm ruined, till I am a pauper.' (146)

In India, woman is considered to be an : 'embodiment of sacrifice, silent suffering, humility, faith and knowledge' (Everett 1981 : 76). MamaPapa are deaf and blind to the needs of their daughter. They forget that Uma is not a body but a soul as well. They, however, feel that if she is kept occupied with one or the other work, she shall not get time to think about her personal dreams, she shall not cherish dreams at all :

> All morning MamaPapa have found things for Uma to do. It is as if Papa's retirement is to be spent in this manner — sitting on the red swing in the veranda with Mama, rocking, and finding ways to keep Uma occupied. (133)

The dreams of a free existence are not unknown or unimagined for Uma. The fact that Moyna Joshi is pursuing a career in Delhi, incites in her an aspiration to make a career, to leave home and to soar high. But her wings have been so badly and pre-maturely clipped, that she can simply flutter her wings, but cannot fly. Aeons of dumb, docile existence renders women incapable to act. They are trained simply to show obeisance to the orders of their rulers. They sulk, they struggle but they are never freed of their meaningless existence as secondary to their masters.

> These troubling, secret possibilities now entered Uma's mind — as Mama would have pointed out had she known — whenever Uma was idle. They were like seeds dropped on the stony, arid land that Uma inhabited. Sometimes, miraculously, they sprouted forth the idea : run away, escape. But Uma could not visualise escape in the form of a career. What was a career? She had no idea. (131)

The romantic poetry of Ella Wheeler Wilcox opens up 'magic casements' before Uma. She is filled with the courage to rebel. But her timid ever-servile soul does not support her rebellion and at the most she registers her anger through an 'angry look at the door' when Mama knocks : 'She hears the door splintering, waits for it to give way, till it does, she will not move. She tightens her hold on the book' (136). Uma's existence has been reduced into an unfed servant who has so many duties but no rights.

II

The novel is certainly Uma's story, but Uma is a helpless member of an orthodox family that is again set in the parochial society. The patriarch happens to be the unchallenged ruler here. He holds the rein and commands all members and all activities inside the family. He has to cater only to the physical needs of the members, emotionally they are not expected to be alive. It is supposed that all members must ally their joys with the happiness of the patriarch. Like a truly devoted servant they are expected to work for his comforts and instead of expecting gratefulness from his side, they should rather feel privileged to serve him. Engels in his *Origin of Species* points out that the very concept of family is based on the presumption that wife belongs to husband. He says that the Latin word 'family' means the total number of slaves belonging to one man. The woman is 'given' in marriage and then she becomes 'his' to command. This sense of belonging is not mutual — husbands do not belong to their wives. Papa believes in the concept of male-superiority and is immodest enough to flaunt it at every opportunity. He is the very epitome of male-chauvinism. Feminists all over condemn this attitude which holds men as 'absolute' and women as 'subjects.' This is precisely what we see in MamaPapa's family. Papa exercises his authority at every little opportunity. Every activity, every moment of life is well within the grip of Papa. A family outing on Sunday evening turns out to be more of an exercise under the strict control of Papa and less of a pleasure trip.

Papa has two daughters but the desire for a son keeps troubling the patriarch. When Mama becomes pregnant for the third time, she has two grown up daughters and out of shame she wants to abort it. But the very thought that women have a right over their bodies is considered preposterous in a patriarchal society. This is what Kate Millett calls *Sexual Politics* 'whereby one group of persons is controlled by another' (Millett 1969 : 23). In a male-dominated society women must always be prepared to allow their husbands to use their bodies for whatever purpose they desire. The perfect one-ness of MamaPapa is disturbed when Mama refuses to oblige. But the tyrant wins again :

> Mama was frantic to have it terminated. She had never been more ill, and would go through hellfire, she wept, just to stop the nausea that tormented her. But Papa set his jaws. They had two daughters, yes, quite grown-up as anyone could see, but there was no son. Would any man give up the chance of a son? (16)

The irony of all this lies in the fact that the woman forgets all humiliation that she was subjected to. After the birth of the son,

Mama again becomes one with Papa. Not only does she forgive the patriarch but also she joins him in his elation at the birth of a son. Mama takes pride in the fact that she has bred a son and for this heroic exploit she is ever grateful to the husband :

> He had not only made her his wife, he had made her the mother of his son. What honour, what status. Mama's chin lifted a little into the air, she looked around her to make sure everyone saw and noticed. She might have been wearing a medal. (31)

III

Feminists all over blame not only male-possessiveness and chauvinism but also female reluctance, easy acquiescence and lethargy for the bad shape that women-existence is in. Male-gods are the unchallengeable legislators of a patriarchal society and women join them in their pride which makes the matters worse. Mama leaves all thinking and decision-making part for Papa. She simply obeys him and takes pride in her servility. This is quite common on the Indian scene but Desai explores the essential oneness of two apparently different cultures. In India Mama shows mute obedience to Papa and follows all his whims and caprices meekly and in Massachusetts, Mrs. Patton shows similar servile attitude. In a country of supposedly strong and independent women Mrs. Patton has made compromises over every small matter. She is not free even in her choice of food. An ardent vegetarian, she has meekly taken to non-vegetarian food because Mr. Patton feels that that is the only kind of food. All her life Mrs. Patton yearned for vegetarian food but out of fear of disturbing the peace of her home, she did not do anything about it. Though she acutally despises meat, in her effort to maintain equilibrium in this strained atmosphere, Mrs. Patton pretends as if she enjoys eating meat prepared by her husband. She confides in Arun :

> I've always hated eating meat — oh, that red, raw stuff, the smell of it! I've always, always disliked it — but never could — never knew how — you know, my family wouldn't have liked it. (179)

She loves vegetables and fruits and finally when she discovers a food-companion in Arun, she is rejoiced no end. This leads to another imbalance in her life. She starts enjoying shopping at the food mart and develops an abnormal flare for it. The lady seems to be craving for an opportunity to shop for food, as Mr. Patton and Rod eat meat only and Melanie has taken to nuts and candies as fish takes to water. When she reminisces about the good old days when she had to buy a lot of food for her family, she seems like a little girl talking about her most cherished dream :

> You should have seen the way I'd load a shopping cart when the children were small. I'd have Melanie sitting up here on the shelf, and there'd be such a heap of groceries under her, she'd have to stick her feet right up on top (196).

It seems that the lady has been starving for real food, and when she gets someone to shop for she makes the most of it. She wears T-shirts with the legend 'Born to Shop' and seems in full control of the situation while in the market. It is hard to believe that at home she is the same, lady with her 'tentativeness and timidity' (183). The seemingly independent woman was so much in awe of her husband that she is 'apologetic and deceitful' when gingerly she announces her decision to 'give vegetarian food a try' (185). Though the cultures, the setting, the socio-familial values are different, the reaction of the patriarch is everywhere the same. Mr. Patton's reaction to his wife's vegetarianism is one of indifference, 'as if he had simply not heard, or understood' (185). Arun notices this one-ness : 'his father's expression, denying any opposition, despair, all seem to him a mirror reflection of it' (185). In contrasted affinity we find the subversive forces working against women both in the parochial Indian society as well as the comparatively free Western society.

IV

Melanie Patton is again a study in psychology. Like Uma this girl also becomes the victim of parental indifference. Her need and thirst for a little love and affection is as intense as that of Uma but unfortunately it is as much in vain as that of her Indian counterpart. On the Indian scene a normal, healthy Uma becomes a patient of Globus hystericus (Hysteria) and on the Western side the insatiated desire for parental affection and attention, makes Melanie a victim of anorexia and bulimia. The novelist writes :

> Then Arun does see a resemblance to something he knows : a resemblance to the contorted face of an enraged sister who, failing to express her outrage against neglect, against misunderstanding, against inattention to her unique and singular being and its hungers, merely spits and froths in effectual protest. How strange to encounter it here, Arun thinks, where so much is given, where there is both licence and plenty (214).

Melanie's alienation from her family points out the essential hollowness of the so-called developed world. Despite all efforts on the part of Mrs. Patton, Melanie remains hungry biologically as well as emotionally. She herself does not know what she wants and keeps venting her anger on her poor mother.

V

Apart from Uma and Melanie, Mira Masi, Mama, Aruna and Anamika make the feminist study complete by presenting various aspects of feminism. Mira Masi is the prototype of an Indian widow : '...quite alone, safe in her widow's white garments, visiting one place of pilgrimage after another like an obsessed tourist of the spirit' (38). All these women have their own hungers (fasting) and all of them crave for a little satiation (feasting). Aruna is what feminists label a truly 'feminine' woman (Shiela Rowbotham). She has no ambition apart from winning a suitable coveted groom for herself by dint of her beauty and coquetry. Since Anita Desai is concerned more with the "exploration of the inner sensibility rather than the outer world of action," (Iyengar 1973 : 392) all her characters merit interpretation from the psychosomatic perspective. As a child Aruna has been a mute witness to her father's hilarity at the birth of a male child. His shameless display of ecstasy had one effect on Uma and altogether different effect on Aruna. Her show of beauty and her coquetry are simply a result of that impact. It is her unique way to show her superiority, it is what may safely be called her self-assertion. This superiority complex becomes strong and takes root as she enters into marriage with Arvind and moves on to a better, richer and more fashionable world of Bombay. The hurt left on her heart since childhood, pushes her towards the quest for a flawless world. The novelist herself writes :

> Clearly Aruna had a vision of a perfect world in which all of them — her own family as well as Arvind's — were flaws she was constantly uncovering and correcting in her quest for perfection. (109)

Not all women are Aruna, most of them are born with a stamp of ill-luck on their foreheads. The tragedy of such women is caused by the fact of their birth in a patriarchal society which fails to respect women as individuals. The lot of women is no way better than that of tragic hero — even the most perfect of them is crushed and doomed. However, there is one clear difference — in women's case 'Hamertia' happens to be no fatal flaw of their own but the bare fact that they belong to the female sex. Anamika — the lovely, intelligent and modest cousin of Uma — presents an example of sheer sacrifice of young, talented lives at the altar of the norms of a male-dominated society. Anamika has all that it takes to go places :

> She was simply lovely as a flower is lovely, soft, petal-skinned, bumblebee-eyed, pink-lipped, always on the verge of bubbling dove-like laughter, loving smiles, and with a good nature like a radiance about her. Wherever she was, there was peace, contentment, well being. (67)

She is not only lovely but also good at studies. She wins a scholarship to Oxford but her parents look upon the letter of acceptance as a trump card which shall be useful in their search for a husband for her. It is this letter of acceptance only that brings about her nemesis. Her scholarship wins for her a husband, who is not only superb but he is also aware of his superb-ness. He does not care a straw for Anamika. He has a mother-fixation and has no time or attention to waste on his wife. Marriage according to Kate Millett is a game of 'power-politics.' Men marry, not because they need a companion or a soul-mate but because marriage gives them a licence to show power. Thus politics enters into marriages. Anamika is also an instrument for her husband 'to enhance his superiority to other men' (70). Though there is no love for her, he does not waste time before impregnating her as a means to crush her even more. But the pregnancy ends in abortion as she is beaten by the mother-in-law. The agony of a woman who is trapped in a wrong marriage is not realised by members of her own race. Though Anamika is experiencing hell, even her own parents do not interfere, neither do they want her back in their home. Anamika's sad saga is a strong statement against a cruel, apathetic society which does not care for lives, instead it gives more importance to its customs and rules. Uma, in her innocence, keeps hoping that Anamika shall be sent back to her mother and all will be well. But she is reproached by her mother with these words : 'You are so silly, Uma. How can she be happy if she is sent home? What will people say? What will they think?' (71). It is this fear of society that leads to the loss of many unfortunate lives. It is this unwillingness to act that results in Anamika's death — rather murder at the hands of her husband and mother-in-law. It is the irony of this unfeeling society that even her death fails to cause a stir or to shake the souls in slumber. They are resigned to their lot. Desai's tone becomes satirical here :

> What the husband said was that he had been away on a business trip and returned only that afernoon on hearing the news.
>
> What the mother-in-law said was that she always had Anamika sleep beside her, in her room, as if she were a daughter, her own child. Only that night Anamia had insisted on sleeping in her own room. She must have planned it, plotted it all.
>
> What Anamika's family said was that it was fate, God had willed it and it was Anamika's destiny.
>
> What Uma said was nothing. (151)

A promising life is reduced to ashes and people who form society still talk instead of taking action. This lethargy and inertia on the part of women has contributed a lot towards the atrophy.

Fasting, Feasting is an indictment against men who believe in holding their women in their grip, it is a statement against women who take pride in their servility, it is again an indictment against men who trade in marriages as a means of increasing money and power, it is a strong criticism against women who, like fish, devour their own frail sisters, above all *Fasting, Feasting* is a plea from a woman in favour of her less fortunate counterparts. It is a strong statement against male-chauvinism, famale apathy and reluctance and it is a woman's voice for freedom and emancipation.

WORKS CITED

De Beauvoir, Simone, 1953. *The Second Sex.* Trans. and ed. H.M. Parshley. Harmondsworth : Penguin, 1983.

Desai, Anita, 1999. *Fasting, Feasting.* London : Chatto and Windus.

Engels, Frederic, 1884. *The Origin of the Family, Private Property and the State.* Moscow : Progress, 1972.

Everett, Jana Matson, 1981. *Women and Social Change in India.* New Delhi : Heritage.

Millett, Kate, 1969. *Sexual Politics.* London : Rupert Hart-Davis, 1971.

Srinivas Iyengar, K.R., 1973. *Indian Writing in English.* New Delhi : Heritage.

Showalter, Elaine, 1989. "Introduction : The Rise of Gender" in Showalter, Elaine, (ed.), *Speaking of Gender.* New York : Routledge.

13

Anita Desai's Short Stories : A Study of *Diamond Dust*

—Basavaraj Naikar

ANITA DESAI, who is basically known as an Indian English woman-novelist, has now published her *Diamond Dust*, a collection of nine short stories. As in here novels, she has exhibited here creative talent in the short stories also. One of the striking features of her writing happens to be her typically feminine point of view, which is expressed through her microscopic observation of life in a very subtle and lyrical language. Whether the setting is Indian, Canadian or British, she has a remarkable power of evoking the atmosphere in a photographic but poetic way. Like a good story teller, she selects a single event or thematic unit and explores its intricacies and highlights its significance in a very subtle manner. Like a goldsmith or an embroiderer, she deals with superfine aspects of life with a microscopic vision. Her stories, therefore, add to the beauty and richness of the genre of Indian short story.

In the first story entitled, "Royalty," the authoress picturizes the contrast between east and west, poetic and prosaic life and nostalgic attachment to one's past. The protagonist of the story, Raja has returned to India from California where he teaches Sanskrit and composes poetry. Now, he is returning from South India to Delhi in a train. Though he is used to flying in America, he prefers to travel by train. His sister Sarla does not understand why he prefers the tedious train journey. Raja has a deep nostalgic attachment to things Indian. That is the reason why he dresses himself in a South Indian *dhoti* and shirt and travels in train to Delhi in order to relive his past and renew his relation with Indian reality and see some (subtle and higher) beauty even in drab and ugly things. Raja easily brings Raja Rao or Ramaswamy to our mind. Sarla who is a practical woman comparatively fails to understand Raja's poetic approach to life. Raja who believes in unity of being, laughs at the double standards of Ravi (Sarla's husband) who dresses himself in tweed suit and hats and pretends to be a patriot. Raja finds spiritual peace in his nostalgic engagement with India. He visits the tomb of Nizamuddin and seems to be deeply moved by it. Similarly he enjoys poetic trance in the observation of the beauty of the Himalayas. Endowed as he is with a poetic and philosophical sensibility, he can not only see but also show to others extraordinary beauty in things ordinary. He enjoys the Indian music with real gusto. Thus, his visit to India enables him to have an intense poetic ecstasy and share it with others. Perhaps there is no greater royalty than the rich artistic experience one undergoes. Anita Desai, thus, explores the psyche of an artist by contrasting it with that of the ordinary ones.

"Winterscape" delineates the widening gap between people of different generations and cultures resulting in a sense of alienation and lack of communication. The story highlights the contrast between Hindu culture and Christian culture. Whereas in Hindu culture filial bonds transcend the barriers of technical relationships of kinship, in Christian (and Western) culture, they are restricted by technical bonds. Whereas Hindu culture believes in a collective happiness, Christian (Western) culture believes in the individual happiness. This contrast is brought out in a subtle fashion by the writer. In a Hindu family there are two sisters, Asha and Annapurna (or Anu). Asha, the elder sister gets married, but does not have any issue. A little later Anu, the younger sister also gets married and has a child named Rakesh in course of time. The childless Asha nourishes Anu's child very affectionately and experiences the joy of surrogate motherhood. Anu gives her child to the care of Asha happily and willingly. Meanwhile, Asha's husband dies most unexpectedly in a gun-accident. This event brings the two sisters emotionally closer. As the child Rakesh grows into a youngman, he cannot differentiate between his mother and aunt on account of their equal affection for him. He, therefore, thinks that he has two mothers instead of one. As he wishes to go to Canada for further education, both the mothers sacrifice their individual pleasure and arrange for the financial support for his education by selling their lands. The Hindu collectivism is contrasted with the Western individualism and selfishness. After completing his education in Canada, Rakesh, like many ambitious Indian youngmen, refuses to return to India and settles down in Canada by marrying a Canadian girl called Berth. When Rakesh wants to invite his two mothers to Canada for a short trip, Berth, like a typical individualistic, Canadian and Western lady, cannot understand how Anu could give her baby to her sister. Berth's mother Doris wonders at Rakesh's having two mothers. That the West cannot understand the East is easily borne out by this situation. The theme of cultural contrast is intersected by that of generation gap and time-gap. When the two mothers go to Canada to stay for a few days with Rakesh and try to remind him of his childhood days, he finds that he has forgotten the past because of the long interval of time as well as his long stay in a foreign land and culture. His growth of personality also adds up to the lack of communication with his two mothers. He is no longer a boy, but a grown up and highly educated man who finds it difficult to communicate with his mothers who are illiterate. Likewise the mothers also feel a sense of alienation. Although Rakesh and Berth try their best to take care of them by buying new cloths for them and taking them out, the two mothers begin to feel bored with the Canadian life and watch the Canadian winter with curiosity. Their watching the winter from the window is captured by Rakesh in his snap of photo. They fall ill because of the cold weather. The winter is not only real but grows metaphorical for them. There is no real communication between the two mothers and their son. Rakesh, therefore, sends them back to India. His wife heaves a sigh of relief when the two mothers leave for India. In this story, Anita

Desai has shown the contrast between an Indian mother and a Canadian mother in a very subtle fashion.

The title story, "Diamond Dust" depicts the theme of unusually intimate relationship between man and animal, between Mr. Das, the protagonist and his pet dog called Diamond. The dog is a terror to the neighbours. People who are scared of it try to avoid going to Mr. Das's compound. The postman tries to avoid it by throwing the mail into the hedge. The dog breaks its chain and goes out for mating bouts with stray bitches and comes back with bloodstains on its genitalia. Mr. Das heaves a sigh of relief on its arrival after the first outing. When it goes out for the second time, it is caught by the police and taken away in the police van. Mr. Das grows anxious about its absence from home and begins to search for it at every possible corner of the city. But when he finds it in the police van, he climbs the rear side of the van and dies when he is jerked back by the vehicle. His deep attachment for the pet dog makes him reckless and costs him his life. Anita Desai seems to teach the lesson that all over — whether of man, or woman, bird or beast — requires some kind of sacrifice.

In "Underground", Jack Higgins and his wife Meg go in a car in search of a hotel on a hot sandy beach. Meg has recently been treated in the hospital and needs rest now. Her husband has brought her in the car in the hot sun and searches for a hotel. But everywhere he gets a negative answer. Finally he has to be satisfied with an underground room. The story is episodic and the motif is not sufficiently clear, although it contains very fine description of the coastal atmosphere.

"The Man Who Saw Himself Drowned", is a psychological fantasy. It shows the death of the protagonist's double by drowning in the river. He attends his double's funeral. The protagonist is nameless. The story has the quality of a fable and is conspicuous for its psychological significance. It easily brings the novels of Kafka to our mind.

"The Artist's Life", presents a picture of the paradox of an artist's life. It shows how an artist has to create beauty in spite of being surrounded by physical and behavioural ugliness. Miss Polly attends a summer school where she is taught by Miss Abigail to paint according to her dreams. Tom is Miss Polly's brother. They have a tenant called Miss Mabel Dodd who is an artist teaching the delinquents in a school. But Miss Mabel, in spite of being an artist, has not cleaned the surroundings of her cabin. Miss Polly's mother is puzzled by Miss Mabel's negligence and wishes to remind her of the need for cleaning. She, therefore, leaves a few garbage cans outside her cabin. Miss Mabel perhaps takes a cue from this and brings a black youth and cleans the surroundings every Sunday. But one day, Miss Polly and her mother are surprised to see that somebody has written 'PIG' on her car with excrement. They cannot guess as to who must have done the filthy thing. The police are called to investigate the matter. It is suspected that one of Miss Mabel's delinquent students or the black youth must have done the heinous thing. This is the fate of an artist dealing with morally ugly people.

In "Tepoztlan Tomorrow," Anita Desai highlights the generation gap between the old and the young, one's nostalgic attachment to one's native city and the progressive deterioration of the city. Louis, son of Teresa, who is the protagonist of this story goes to Tepoztlan and meets Dona Celia. While having his dinner, he inadvertently refers to Pedro and spoils Dona Celia's mood. It is very unpleasant for Dona Celia to remember Pedro who was her suitor but whose family she had disliked. Next morning Dona Celia and her daughter Nadyn complain to Louis about a neighbour who is a professional garbage picker and who disturbs them with the stinking smell and the loud music of radio and TV and by her other dirty habits.

Louis meets his friend Arturo and talks about the past very nostalgically. Arturo invites him to the golf club for having some fun. Then he meets Don Beto who enquires about his thesis and study at the University of Houston and advises him to write polemical articles and to oppose the golf club. Later Lousi goes to the golf club where he sees Alesandro playing guitar and

Arturo. Then he sees some parts of the city, returns to Dona Celia's home and takes his leave with the pretext of continuing his research. The story, thus, shows a picture of decadence of the city in various ways, quite in line with Nirad Chaudhuri's picture of American decadence as part of global decadence.

"Five Hours to Simla or Faisla," is one of the successful stories in this collection because of the clarity of motif in it. It is a humorous story about the adamance of a sardarji causing a good deal of tension to the travellers on the way to Simla. A family is going to Simla in a car. They have to travel another five hours to reach the place. But on the way, they are forced to stop the car as an unexpected difficulty crops up. When the sardarji is driving his truck along the road, some goatherd pelts a stone at his vehicle as a consequence of which the windscreen of his truck is broken. Now the sardarji gets angry, parks his truck across the road thereby blocking the traffic from both sides. He demands compensation for the breakage of his windscreen by the goatherd. There is a traffic jam for two miles. The sardarji sits leisurely on the bridge wall without heeding for the tension of other travellers. They do not know how to tackle him because of his irrational demand. Some people go in search of the goatherd. Some others go to the nearest city to find out a police station. Meanwhile a temporary market gathers there. The members of family feel restless and helpless in the car. Beggars, hawkers, tea-vendors and toy-vendors gather there to make the best of the situation. During the four or five hours of tension and waiting, the members in the car compromise with the situation gradually. Necessity impels them to neglect the ideal of hygiene. They are forced to eat and drink the cheap stuff that is available with the hawkers and vendors. After a long and tedious waiting, they are surprised to see a police van come from a nearby town. All the travellers are expecting an exchange of words between the sardarji and the police officers. But to their surprise, the sardarji, far from asking for any compensation, climbs into his truck, starts it and drives away from there without any demur. The family heave a sigh of relief after great tension. The sardarji's behaviour is, obviously, as adamant as irrational and humorous.

"The Rooftop Dwellers" deals with the problems of a working single woman in Delhi. Moyna is a young lady who has passed her M.A. in English and who wants to earn her livelihood in the metropolitan city of Delhi. She joins as a sub-editor of a literary magazine entitled *Books*. Tara happens to be her senior colleague whose husband Ritwik is a teacher in Jawaharlal Nehru University at Delhi. Moyna cannot afford to hire an expensive house or apartment. Besides, space is a big problem in the overcrowded capital city. Moyna, therefore, hires a rooftop *barsati* and suffers from minimalism, lack of social life and insecurity. She has to get up early in the morning to collect water from the tap as there is no facility for storing it. The owners of the house suspect her character when she brings male friends to her room. Once when she returns in the evening, she is surprised and shocked to learn that the things in her room are stolen by somebody. In course of time she realises the impracticability of running a literary magazine. The politician who is financing the magazine decides to wind it up. Finally Moyna is called by her mother to meet a bridegroom who has returned from America. Though simple, the story throws light upon the contemporary Indian society by highlighting the problems of an unmarried working woman like the financial, social and emotional ones. An educated woman in India has to face many odds in her adventure of achieving her identity. Anita Desai's depiction of women's problems has a ring of authenticity and sympathy.

On the whole, the stories in *Diamond Dust* are written from an omniscient point of view. Out of the nine stories, five are set in Canada and England and four in India. They are conspicuous for their remarkable and microscopic description, evocation of relevant mood and atmosphere and insight into the subtle working of the human mind. Sometimes her virtues become her vices in that the abundance of descriptive element tends to slacken the pace of the stories. As the blurb says, "In this brilliant new collection of funny, sad, compassionate and

Deshpande uses this point of view to present social reality as it is experienced by women. To present the world of mothers, daughters and wives is also to present indirectly the fathers, sons and husbands, the relation between men and women, and between women themselves. In presenting women's point of view Deshpande is mainly interested in the clash of tradition and modernity, as reflected in the generation gap and conflict between women. Her young heroines rebel against the traditional way of life and patriarchal values. Jaya, Sarita and Sumi perceive the structuring of men and women in gendered roles, restricting their human potentiality and fullness. They struggle to transcend the restrictive roles. They rebel, reject and seek freedom from the traditional norms and way of life. Shashi Deshpande's portrayal of the women of different generations presents the world of women divided into the traditional and modern. Her female protagonists are from the middle-class. Besides her class identity, she cannot betray her gender identity. She says, "as writing is born out of personal experience, the fact that I am a woman is bound to surface. Besides, only a woman could write my books — they are written from inside, as it were."

Shashi Deshpande's writing is gender specific. Feminism is at the core of her novels. She deals with a woman's psyche and the way she is made to feel an inferior being, an unwanted child, a burden on the family for instance, Kalyani in *A Matter of Time.* The mother-daughter relationship has an important place in her novels. In *A Matter of Time* Kalyani-Sumi and Sumi-Aru are fascinating relationships. Marginalised men and silent women are depicted in *A Matter of Time.*

A Matter of Time revolves around the absence of the principal character Gopal from his family. He walks out on his wife Sumi and three daughters. This is set against the backdrop of the sad tale of Kalyani and Shripati in the 'Big House.' It is the house to which Sumi returns with Aru, Charu and Seema, when Gopal leaves them. Gopal's absence from the family scene creates unique tension for the various characters. Each one of them tries to find out Gopal's reason. Then there is conjugal

charming stories, Anita Desai shows us ordinary lives in a disconcerting world, where hopes and dreams clash with disappointment and the human spirit shines strongly from India to Canada and England." One cannot but agree with *The Times* which says, "These are stories whose beauty is in the detail, and their knowledge of the human psyche. They sparkle, not with the brash glitter of rhinestones, but with the intenser, more complex fire of real diamonds." Obviously, the stories of *Diamond Dust* add to the beauty and richeness of the genre of Indian English short story.

WORK CITED

Anita Desai, *Diamond Dust*, London : Vintage, 2000.

14

Shashi Deshpande's *A Matter of Time* "As an Exploration of a Woman's Inner Life"

—N.B. Masal

SHASHI DESHAPANDE is one of the famous contemporary Indian novelists in English. She deals with the inner world of the Indian women in her novels. She portrays her heroines in a realistic manner. Basically she writes about the situation of women and their failures in the fast changing socio-economic milieu of India. She writes about the conflict between tradition and modernity in relation to women in the middle class society. A woman is the centre of her fictional world. Her desires, efforts and failures in the traditional Indian Society are the main points in her novels. She makes it clear that hers is not the strident and militant kind of a feminism which sees man as the cause of all troubles. Her depiction of women's world is authentic, realistic and credible. She presents the middle class women in her novels.

The present paper deals with in what way Shashi Deshpande's novel *A Matter of Time* is an exploration of a woman's inner life. Shashi Deshpande's latest novel *A Matter of Time* was published by Penguin Books, India in 1996. Her novels generally explore a woman's psyche. *The Dark Holds No Terror, That Long Silence, The Binding Vine* and *Roots and Shadows* deal with feminist issues Deshpande's latest novel *A Matter of Time* (1996), too, deals with the same subject. Yet a woman's inner life is not the only subject of this novel. Here the inner life of woman emotionally isolated from her family is reflected and

refracted in the embryonic women represented by Deshpande does believe that she is a feminist and are universal. She writes about silent, sobbin mothers, grandmothers, aunts, sisters, grand-aunts, a a whole lot of females. Probably the author herself too many thronging the pages of the novel.

Shashi Deshpande's novels present a social wor complex relationship. Many men and women live to journey across life in their different age groups, c gendered roles. Doubt, anxiety and often a feeling values push characters in her novels to intense self-exa The women are particularly caught in the process of r and rediscovering their own roles, position and relat within their given social world. In the extended fami Shashi Deshpande presents, two or three generatio together. She presents the modern Indian womanhood novels. Her own struggle as a writer to focus on women's problems, and experience is equally symptomatic resistance to feminist expression that prevails in India middle of twentieth century. She tries to distance herself women's lives and point of view through the use of narrative voice. As a woman writer, her dilemma was eith give voice to women's concern and be branded as a wo writer; removed from the mainstream of literary scene, c deny her femininity and write like a man either with the r name or male narrative voice. The live experiences and vi point of women represent after all "one half of humanity." emphatic claim that she is feminist came gradually to her as main literary concern. She admits in an article in the *Time India* that even to myself. I am a feminist (May 10, 199 became, she says, an acceptance of my womanhood as a pos thing, not as a lack. The concerns of women are primarily ir context of the family and the community. Despande has lo into woman's changing perspectives and their search for bon within family as a mode of strength.

relationship between Kalyani and Shripati. The lack of communication between them impinges on the wider issues of patriarchy that influences the successive generations. History has repeated itself in the life of Sumi. But on both occasions Kalyani and Sumi are silent. Kalyani suffers silently. She fears a similar fate to Sumi. Kalyani's fears based on patriarchal oppression that condemns women to the margins of silence. She is made to realize that while losing her son, a male heir, she had abandoned her motherhood as well as her right as a wife. Her punishment is that she has to live with this psychic wound. Really it was not her fault. Her predicament is that the woman's body is not only a text of culture. It is a focus of social control, and the site of violence, exclusion and abuse. In this social construction of body the subject is denied agency and is compelled to accept her passivity. For nearly thirty-five years she remains a second sex, a passive silent sufferer. Her body becomes a 'site of colonizing power.' Kalyani's mother in her childhood blamed Kalyani for not being a son and it is injustice towards females.

Kalyani fears about her daughter, Sumi. In Sumi's life there is a vacuum because of Gopal's abandonment. Sumi tries to find out clues to his probable motives in his past acts and utterances. Gopal said once that *Sa-hriday* in the sense of oneness is an impossible concept. Gopal accepts the traditional Hindu view of marriage where God unites both the hearts. He also believes that the husband and wife are described as two halves of one being. But he realizes that he was failing the idealistic expectations of his marriage. He could not feel himself a *Sa-hriday* with Sumi and was getting out of step with her. The breakdown of Sumi's marriage had circumscribed Sumi in an unexpected condition. Gopal's absence leaves her in a state of vast emptiness. She feels, "I can't find my bearings, there are no markers any more to show me which way I should go." Yet it is from the depth of her despair that she tries to transform her emptiness into meaning in order to redefine her identity. She does not remain a passive mother, but an active agent. We cannot forget that Sumi, like her mother, is a suffering oppressed and wronged woman. Yet she does not question the man, her oppressor.

In the maze of family history, what happens to Sumi and her daughters? Nothing and everything. Nothing because no solution is found to their problem; everything because Sumi and Shripati are killed in an accident. The 'Big House' watches one more generation going down in history and one generation writhing under the impact of a relentless fate.

Sumi's daughter Aru is a rebel. She rebels against her father. She approaches Gopal not expecting sympathy for her or for her mother. She wants to unravel the strange behaviour of her father. She asks Gopal "Why did you get married at all, why did you have children?" Her searching question makes Gopal re-examine his motives in fleeing from the family. Aru is disappointed to see the tragedy of her grandmother and mother. Out of frustration she declares 'I'm never going to get married.' She holds strong views on patriarchy and how women, in general, get victimized as a result of the actions of men. She is critical of Gopal. She wants to see it that Gopal does not go scot free. Aru meets a feminist, Surekha, a lawyer by profession. However the activist lawyer does not find it a case of the usual marital discord.

Shashi Deshpande flashes some light on the cause of women's education and liberation. Then the whole novel is devoted to silent, brooding women, unhappy, yet lively, clinging to their past, yet living in the present. The men do not play an active role in the story. But they are the root cause of all suffering, Gopal and Shripati. Deshpande tries to exonerate the male by bringing in some strong, loving and responsible figures. But they come and go, flitting like shadows. The real balance is tilted by Gopal and Shripati. Gopal's exit reminds us of Anita Desai's protagonist in her story "Surface Texture" and Nirode in *Voices in the City* and Arun Joshi's *Billy Biswas.*

A Matter of Time is a composite study in human relationships. Gopal's absence seems to be similar to the departure of the British masters from India. The most striking example of silence is Kalyani who spends nearly forty years in total silence with her husband, Shripati.

Shashi Deshpande is a woman writer, who writes about women. Most of her writing comes out of her own intense and long suppressed feelings about what it is to be a woman in our society. It comes out of the experience of the difficulty of playing different roles. Her writing comes out of her consciousness of the conflict between her idea of herself as a human being and the idea that society has of her as a woman. As a woman writer she deals with gender-related experiences. Her *That Long Silence* is the most autobiographical novel. She believes that all good writing is socially committed writing. It comes out of a concern for the human predicament. Her wish is to be recognized as a writer who deals with issues that are human and of interest to all humanity.

Shashi Deshpande's novel *A Matter of Time* is a novel of human bonds and bondages. It is a very different reading experience from '*The Binding Vine*.' *A Matter of Time* has elicited a very fine response from foreign readers, Australian, English and American. Gopal-Sumi relationship is the most rewarding thing in it. The mother-daughter relationship is superbly authentic. Human relationship is the main theme of this outstanding novel. In this way, in this novel Shashi Deshpande presents an exploration of woman's inner life.

15

Deconstructing Femininity : A Reading of Namita Gokhale's *Paro : Dreams of Passion*

—Kuldeep Kumar & Gajendra Kumar

DECONSTRUCTION OR Deconstructionist approach came in vogue in France towards the end of sixties and the beginning of seventies. This approach is, in fact, a post-structuralist approach. Structuralist approach aimed at objectivity, technicality, precision and real technical analysis of a text. Structuralists pre-supposed death of the author. They absolutely denied the context which was not tenable. Deconstructionist approach is in fact the reversal of structuralist approach. Whereas the structuralist approach analysed text to bring out a pattern or structure in a work of art, deconstruction focuses on the *'absences'* and *'gaps'* in the text. The former lays bare the present, the latter emphasizes the absent. In this way deconstruction highlights the marginalized in literature. This is why this approach has been so useful in modern feminist criticism.

According to structuralists every word is a sign which is made up of two components — signifier and signified. Signifier is a mark which is either written or spoken and signified is the concept behind it. According to deconstructionists this process does not stop here. Whenever a signifier is broken into its concepts, a new set of signifieds is released. It is just like a chain reaction. This relationship between a signifier and signified is deconstructive in nature. It is not a permanent or final relationship but a temporary, arbitrary and relative one. This relationship can be deconstructed and then again reconstructed. This approach aims neither at construction of a particular meaning nor at destruction of that meaning. Its main argument is that meaning of a particular sign can be deconstructed. There is neither affirmation of a meaning nor negation of a meaning but a constant postponement of meaning is there. The very process in which the relationship between signifier and signified is postponed is deconstructive in nature. According to deconstructionists all cultural, social, literary courses have lost their meanings as they are now open for deconstruction. According to them concepts like goodness, purity, naturalness and truth are arbitrary and tentative. According to Derrida, similar is the case with more abstract and philosophical versions of authority such as "aletheia, transcendentality, consciousness or conscience, God, man and so forth."[1]

All these concepts which were earlier presumed to be self-evident and correct are now bound to be deconstructed. According to Derrida, "since the center does not belong to the totality, the totality has its center elsewhere." It means the center is not the center. The very concept of a center is arbitrary. This center is not "a fixed locus but a function, a sort of nonlocus in which an infinite number of sign-substitutions come into play."[2]

In fact, according to deconstructionists, there is a decentering in the conventional order. Every concept now leads to scepticism. There has been "a dramatic and decisive shift in the old relations to authority. The western mind has gradually learned to accept authority (the 'center') only by investigating to find its underlying 'authority' and then to find its underlying 'authority' of that authority and so on."[3] Derrida and others seem to assert that the full meaning of any word, phrase or text will never simply stop and declare itself for there will always be a further nuance to pursue.

Deconstructionists have been influenced by the great philosopher Nietzche. Nietzche's assertion that the same text authorizes innumerable interpretations : there is no correct interpretation, forms the basic argument of the deconstruction.

The very act of reading imports same meaning in the meaningless text. According to Miller, "Ultimately man finds in things nothing but what he himself has imported into them."[4] Just like Nietzche, Paul de Man asserts that a text says one thing and does another.... First a text has a meaning or a given and somewhat static significance; next the text 'asserts' or 'performs' a quite different meaning as if to constitute a different 'text' inconsistent with the first.

Deconstructive approach follows from the basic ideas of Derrida about textuality, undecidability and strategy. Textuality is a subject to a certain instability or undecidability. That is text of any sort will produce meanings but since the production of meaning cannot be assisted through a relationship with absolute referents, textuality will always be in progress and unfinished and thus undecidable. Another important issue for deconstruction is strategy which aims at reversal of western culture's important hierarchies such as male/female, truth/error, philosophy/literature, speech/writing, and seriousness/play.

So the main emphasis of deconstruction is on the lack of any final meaning in any text or any concept. All these things are arbitrary and can be deconstructed. Just like Derrida, Miller asserts that text is nothing more than "innocent marks on a page."[5] These marks don't carry any fixed meaning in themselves. The very act of reading imports some meaning in those marks. So the meanings assigned to those marks are arbitrary and are not final. The moment we come to know the meaning of a sign it slips away. As M.H. Abrams points out that while interpreting a text, when we are about to grasp a particular meaning "the bottom drops away,"[6] and we can never get any final meaning of the text. But deconstruction is confined not only to the literary texts but as pointed out earlier, this approach can be applied to all the concepts whether they are social, philosophical or literary. All these concepts are arbitrary and hence open to deconstruction. All dichotomies in the areas of culture, literature, arts are tentative. Same is the case with gender dichotomies. Categories like 'man' and 'woman', 'male' and 'female', masculine' and 'feminine', are all tentative. We cannot derive a final meaning out of this sort of categorisation. All these canons are arbitrary and open to deconstruction.

Now the question arises why this sort of differentiation is done at all? Why the males are associated with concepts like 'masculinity' and females with 'femininity?' Masculinity has always been "associated with power, independence, self-assertion, activity, domination, etc."[7] On the other hand femininity is always "associated with weakness, helplessness, dependence, passivity, docility, subservience and complacence."[8]

Thus, femininity, womanhood is a concept which has its roots in patriarchy which is a historical and social system. According to deconstructionists all systems and concepts are arbitrary, tentative and open to deconstruction. Thus femininity, which aimed at docility, modesty, chastity, sacrifice on the part of women, is also open to deconstruction.

In *Paro,* Namita Gokhale has tried to deconstruct the concept of femininity. Paro, the central character, is shown to be a rebel who revolts against the social and moral codes assigned to a woman. She is neither chaste nor submissive as is expected of a woman. She denies social codes, traditions, authority and all those things which force a woman to become a prioner of her own sex. According to deconstructionists all the terms related to femininity are arbitrary and man made and cannot be taken as final. Femininity in itself has no meaning. It has been assigned a particular meaning by a male dominated society which can be deconstructed.

Just in the beginning of the novel, Priya, the narrator of the novel, gives us a very unfeminine picture of Paro. Paro was going to get married to B.R., who was Priya's boss. Priya was invited to the marriage party where she was shocked to see the unfeminine appearance of Paro as a bride. She was not at all resembling any traditional Indian bride. A bride behaving in such a careless manner and taking wine is no doubt against the concept of femininity. Paro seems to have revolted against the social codes and traditions but through this she has been able to get an individuality of her own. Instead of becoming repulsive she becomes a sort of attraction for others.

Paro's outgoing nature helped her to become a social celebrity very soon. She came out of the areas which were allotted to women and succeeded in making a place for her in male dominated society. Paro came out of the traditional image of a woman, who was forced to remain inside the house where she was expected to do nothing else than household chores, child-bearing and child-rearing.

Paro's way of speaking became an obsession for Priya. She tells, "Subconsciously I would find myself mouthing her words; phrases that were not mine would spill unsuspecting from my lips; gestures that were hers would enact themselves in involuntary mine" (p. 16). Priya always fantasised herself being Paro. Paro had been able to make such a place in society that girls like Priya started taking her as their model. Paro's way of getting herself dressed up was also non-traditional. Unlike a traditional Indian woman who is wrapped in a sari, she preferred wearing dresses like "a black sequinned off shoulder kurta, which left one shoulder completely bare, almost naked" (p. 24). Priya tried to follow Paro and started smoking, visiting beauty parlours and wearing modern dresses. But Suresh, Priya's husband, objects to it. He wants to see Priya as a typical Indian woman, dressed up in saris only. Unlike Paro, Priya retreated back into her Indian wife. But Paro represented a liberated woman who is not ready to follow the social codes.

After some time, Paro leaves her husband and starts living with 'Bucky' Bhandpur. She liberated herself from "marriage and convention" and still believed that "she is as young and desirable as she ever was" (p. 27). She had left her husband and was "living in open adulterous sin with 'Bucky' Bhandpur. But she was not at all ashamed of it. Priya describes Paro's new role as a woman who has risen even above liberation or emancipation. She says, "Life has not tired her — she is undiminished" (p. 28). Paro's relation with 'Bucky' Bhandpur does not last for a longer period. She leaves 'Bucky' very soon and thus becomes a liberated woman who has "left a husband and a lover," and has "a small son of ambiguous parentage" (p. 28). Thus she senies the social and moral codes and dares to have a child whose father is unknown. Again she has revolted against the norms of femininity where a woman is supposed to be chaste. She is nothing more than a prostitute but we cannot call her a prostitute as there is no final meaning in anything. Namita Gokhale has presented an image of Paro which is non-traditional. Paro has denied authority, tradition, social and moral codes and has made a place for her in the society.

Suresh, Priya's husband, entered into Paro's life when she was facing a number of legal problems. On the face of it, Suresh was using her contacts for making more clients but in fact Paro had attracted Suresh as well. She started visiting Priya's house and it was during one of her visits that she told Priya about her tragedy. Her tale of woes started when she was raped by her art master. No doubt, Paro became a victim of the lust of a male but all this seems to be a mere formula as she loved every moment of her so called rape. She herself says, "Funny thing is that I wasn't raped, I loved every moment of it" (p. 33). So Paro is no doubt a woman of loose morals who has no sense of guilt, or shame for her being so. To an outsider, Paro's rape is a ghastly incident. But quite paradoxically Paro enjoys every moment of the 'operation.' The notion behind a 'rape' stands deconstructed here.

Paro never felt a sense of shame in talking about sex or anything which is obscene. Paro talks about such things which were considered as taboos to be discussed. No doubt this is a feminist point of view but it is not a healthy way in which Paro has tried to achieve this. She is told of having relationships with a young boy called Avinendra, who is son of the Industry Minister. He considered Paro to be a free woman, a real individual. Once in a hotel while taking dinner with others he declares, "'Now this lady...is a real individual. She has the courage of her convictions. She is not a kept woman; she is free'" (p. 37). On hearing this, Priya finds a ray of triumph in Paro's eyes who was "now the freewoman, symbol and prototype of emancipation and individuality" (p. 48). Soon after Paro herself declares, " 'I am myself, and no one else. I depend on nobody. I am my own person' " (p. 48). Paro has thus succeeded to come out of the stereo-type image of women where they were believed to be biologically unfit to assume responsibility and hence needed male protection and guidance. Paro need not depend on anybody.

She was making all this drama to capture the attention of others just like a whore. She was very much enthusiastic about showing off her skills to people around her. As Priya tells, "Her enthusiasm was almost a primitive exhibitionism, actually she would show off her skills to all and sundry, quite unmindful of the suitability of the occasion" (p. 61). Her behaviour is obviously against the norms of femininity. But Paro was not at all embarrassed or ashamed of her act. She simply said, " 'We were just talking about Yoga' " (p. 63). But the other people attending the party were really shocked to see such an unfeminine woman.

When Lenin wins a lottery of five lakhs, Paro's perversities awaken again. This time she takes Shambhu Nath Misra into her clutches. In her very first encounter with him "She was responding feverishly, obscenely, like a cat in heat" (p. 77). She never liked to be tied up with a single man. She went to America with Shambhu Nath Misra but her passion was spent when she returned. Once again she goes back to 'Bucky' Bhandpur. In the mean time when Avinendra finds Paro growing indifferent towards him, he plans to marry. After his marriage, Paro feels alone and so she joins the theatre with the help of a young director Krishen Narain Singh. She plays the role of Clytemnestra, who is shown to be a passionate and strong woman with a creepy husband. She kills her husband and in retaliation is killed by her son. It is here that Paro attacks male chauvinism. She says " 'It's all the male types, it's because of the social framework. You know all the fucking freedom of men, and none for women' " (p. 105). In order to get equality with men she revolted against all the moral codes and virtually deconstructed the norms of femininity.

Once more incident which depicts Paro's daring and unpredictable nature is when she marries, once again, a European Cinema celebrity, Loukas Leoros. He was a homosexual and could never satisfy Paro. She confessed " 'I feel like a cat on a hot tin roof; I'm in heat; I need a man; And Loukas, as we all know, is a woman' " (p. 145).

Namita Gokhale perhaps poses a question to the very concepts of femininity and feminism. In denying the social codes of femininity, Paro had tried to achieve the equality and individuality. Paro, no doubt, asserts her femininity but at the same time she does not behave in a masculine manner. But the type of feminism which Paro propagates is self-destructive as it does not lead to any harmonious relationships between man and woman which should be the ultimate aim of feminism.

Through Paro, Namita Gokhale has deconstructed the very concept of femininity which aimed at women to be docile, submissive, chaste and modest. Paro has, in fact, denied all these codes but in a very unhealthy manner. It is quite easy to dismiss Paro as a 'bad' or 'fallen woman' in a casual critical appreciation of the novel. By reading the novel deconstructively, a perceptive reader/critic may gain new and fresh insights about its characters and events since the deconstructive critical endeavour does not accept a label or a concept at its face value. It brings to the fore what is generally, hither to hidden from our view. Paro, deconstructively speaking, is neither a 'bad' or a 'good woman.' She is just what she is and what she wants to be.

REFERENCES

1. Quoted in Robert Con Davis, "The Post-Structuralist 'Texte'," *Contemporary Literary Criticism : Modernism Through Post-Structuralism,* p. 409.
2. *Ibid.,* p. 395.
3. Con Davis, pp. 409-10.
4. Quoted in Abrams, p. 430.

5. Quoted in Abrams, p. 433.
6. *Ibid.*, p. 435.
7. Iqbal Kaur, "Femininity and Feminist Literature," *Feminist Revolution and Kamla Das's My Story* (Patiala : Century Twentyone Publications, 1992), p. 13.
8. *Ibid.,* p. 13.

16

The Magic Wand of Arundhati Roy : The Strategy of Words in *The God of Small Things*

—Asha Choubey

THERE HAVE been novels by great writers, with superb style and good themes, there have also been novels by not so great writers with good themes but ordinary narration, but there has seldom been a novel from an obscure writer with superb theme and equally superb style to match. *The God of Small Things* falls precisely into the last category. It is a nice, touching tale told superbly by an ordinary woman who shot to limelight on account of being the writer of *The God of Small Things. A* disinterested architect-cum-free lance script writer became a renowned writer when she published *The God of Small Things.* The novel has been acclaimed highly as a 'brilliant novel' and even 'a contemporary classic.' Mainly the story of Ammu, the novel takes its readers to heights of human passions and arouses the emotions of love, fear, anger, indignation, pity as not many works do. The three-generation story becomes an experience for a sensitive reader and one wonders what is so new about it. It is a poignant story of the plight of women in a parochial, patriarchal society. We have several other novels centering around such themes, yet the impact of *The God of Small Things* is unique. It is a classic which is here to stay, to remain etched in the memory for a long time to come. It maintains its charm and enamours the readers at every subsequent reading. A major part of its charisma comes from novelty of language. Roy demonstrates a perfect command over English and handles words with utmost eclat. The purpose of this paper is to bring out the charm of this book which lies in a great part, in its deft — rather wonderful handling of words.

I

A very simple and thin story-line has been woven into a charming master-piece, not so much by any other device, as by its language. Lynn Altenbernd and Leslie L. Lewis observe :

> The author's word choice (whether formal or informal, literal or metaphorical), the sonority or flatness of sentence form, and the allusiveness of his diction are all elements of language that help to shape the significance of the story. (Altenbernd *et al.* 1977, 73).

Words become larger than life when Roy uses them in the uppercase or capitals. Ammu has two children Rahel and Estha who are not only twins, they are emotionally inseparable as well. One heart seems to beat in two bodies. The story begins when Rahel comes back to Ayemenem after a long time marked by Ammu's death and Estha's return from his father. Ammu — their mother was divorced and the children were divided between parents — Estha went to the father and Rahel to Ammu. Looking from this juncture, those early days of childhood seem blessed. After a long period of separation, dejection and desolation, when Rahel remembers those days she feels :

> In those early amorphous years when memory had only just begun, when life was full of beginnings and no Ends, and Everything was for ever, Esthappen and Rahel thought of themselves together as Me, and separately, individually, as We or Us (Roy 1997 : 2 All subsequent references are from this edition).

The use of capitals inside the sentences lends new vision, newer insight to the words. None else but Rahel only could think like this. Such sentences create unique effect and the reader feels as if it is through a telescope that he can read the influx — the luminous halo inside Rahel's in mind. Such uses lend charm to the stream of consciousness technique and take it more potent, more powerful. Roy is as adventurous with words as Emily Dickinson and e. ecummings and does in fiction what they did in poetry. Emphasis is put on words by the use of capitals within sentences. Baby Kochamma is a snob and a hater of communism. She is whimsical and takes pride in the Ayemenem house which rightfully belongs to Esthappen and Rahel. She believes in keeping all her possessions under lock and key. Her love for privacy and fear of outsiders is brought out by the use of capitals. She opened the Windows only 'for a Breath of Fresh Air. To Pay for the Milk — To Let Out a Trapped Wasp.' (28)

Rahel is always too full of hopes but almost all hopes of hers end in disaster. She hopes that the railway level-crossing gate would not close and they would not be late for the show of 'Sound of Music.' But the gate goes down before their eyes and they have to wait. The whole idea is to strike home the point that Rahel has all unrequired and unnecessary hopes and that it is simply because of this incorrigible optimism that she faces disappointment ultimately. This idea is conveyed beautifully and subtly through capitals. She had not learnt to control her 'Hopes' yet. Estha said that it 'was a Bad Sign.' (58)

Roy has made a brilliant use of similes and metaphors. Though Louella Lobo Prabhu has a different opinion :

> However, after a few more pages were read, I found the endless heaping of similes and metaphors, a self-conscious and tedious exercise. In describing a single item of scenery with not one, but loads of metaphor, one feels the author is practising the dictum, "Nothing succeeds like excess." (Dec. 1997 : 12)

While going to watch the movie *The Sound of Music*, Ammu's family is caught up in a communist procession. Rahel spies Velutha — the paravan servant of the family — amid the procession, holding a banner and she speaks out loudly about it. Valutha happens to be Ammu's paramour. Ammu, knowing that he may land up in trouble for being a part of this procession tries to stop Rahel but the child would not understand. The look in

Ammu's eyes terrifies her, once she has spilled the beans. Rahel could not understand that look till she meets an insane woman on board a local train in New York. The eyes of this woman seem to convey everything to Rahel and the stony look in Ammu's eyes becomes clear to her that day. It is through wonderful use of metaphors that Roy describes the striking similarity of the expression in eyes of these two women :

> Memory was that woman on the train. Insane in the way she sifted through dark things in a closet and emerged with the most unlikely ones — a fleeting look, a feeling. The smell of smoke. A windscreen wiper. A mother's marble eyes. Quite sane in the way she left huge tracts of darkness veiled. Unremembered. (72)

Dr. Prabhu's assertions notwithstanding, Roy's similes and metaphors create atmosphere, they build pictures.

Chacko has a knack of simplifying most complicated ideas with the help of similes and metaphors. He defines history for the twins in these words :

> He explained to them that history was like an old house at night. With all the lamps lit. And ancestors whispering inside. To understand history, Chacko said, 'we have to go inside and listen to what they're saying. And look at the pictures on the wall. And smell the smells.' (52)

The story of creation is told to the children by Chacko through similes and metaphors and instead of making the matter tedious and complicated metaphorical explanation makes it as easy and clear as can be :

> It has taken the whole of the Earth woman's life for the earth to become what it was. For the oceans to part. For the mountains to rise. The earth woman was eleven years old, Chacko said, when the first single-cell organisms appeared. The first animals, creatures like worms and jelly-fish, appeared only when she was forty. She was over forty-five — just eight months — when dinosaurs roamed the earth.

History has been used in the sense of the inevitable.

> History's smell.
>
> Like old roses on a breeze.
>
> It would lurk forever in ordinary things. In coat-hangers. Tomatoes. In the tar on the roads. In certain colours. In the plates at a restaurant. In the absence of words. And the emptiness in eyes. (55)

History is the motivating force behind all human actions. We falsely believe, we make history in fact the corollary is true that history uses human beings as instruments. It is history in whose hands we are, 'like flies to wanton boys' :

> His feet walked him to the river. As though they were the leash and he were the dog.
>
> History walking the dog. (288)

The History house is later acquired by a hotelier and transformed into an expensive hotel. This total metamorphosis is :

> The humbling of old communists. The slow death of dancers. The toy histories that rich tourists came to play with. (306)

It is in the History house that the love story of Ammu flourishes and it is there only that their love is nipped in the bud. History house is not a mute witness instead it takes a character as gigantic as powerful as gods, as furies, as Hardy's Egdon Heath.

> What Vellya Paapen didn't know was that Kari Saipu's house was the History House. And that inside, map-breath'd ancestors with tough toe-nails whispered to the lizards on the wall. That history used the back verandah to negotiate its terms and collect its dues. That default lead to dire consequences. That on the day History picked to square its books, Estha would keep the receipt for the due that Velutha paid. (199)

Most beautiful, nonpareil is the description of the mating of Velutha and Ammu. If suggestiveness is the hallmark of good poetry, it is here that it is in plenty :

> Clouded eyes held clouded eyes in a steady gaze and a luminous woman opened herself to a luminous man. She

> was as wide and deep as a river in spate. He sailed on her waters. She could feel him moving deeper and deeper into her. Frantic. Frenzied. Asking to be let in further. Further. Stopped only by the shape of her. The shape of him. And when he was refused, when he had touched the deepest depths of her, with sobbing, shuddering sigh, he drowned. (336-37)

Estha becomes absolutely silent after his re-return from his father. He stops reacting to anything. Though life has certainly not been fair to him, he becomes too numb to complain. It is a kind of stupor that seems to overpower him. The idea has been beautifully conveyed :

> It was human history, masquerading as God's Purpose, revealing herself to an under-age audience.
>
> ....
>
> After all, they were not battling an epidemic. They were merely inoculating a community against an outbreak. (309)

III

Words seem to be toys in Roy's hands. She plays upon them with the ease of a master. She twists them, breaks them, joins them, hyphenates them, italicises them, tosses them as she would, creates music out of them and solves her purpose. Words have been used as wonderfully as here. Her aim is to be articulate and like a magician she takes words out of her bag and they obey her command. If she wants them to hang in the air, they do so, if she wants to cut through them, they allow her, if she would duplicate them, they carry her behest. She has to utter abracadabra, and there they are, waiting for her next command. Chacko's anglophile attitude and lifestyle have been seen through different angles and they have been variously described. From Chacko he becomes Chacko of Oxford (223). Chacko is a professed communist but only theoretically. As far as imbibing the communist ideals is concerned, he is not even remotely a follower of Marx. It is because of his pseudo-Marxism that Mammachi and Baby Kochamma call him 'Man of the Masses.'

He likes dressing up as a sahib and his English suit becomes 'What happened to our Man of the Masses suit.' (173)

IV

The test of language is its ability to convey the intents most easily, clearly and above all naturally. If *The God of Small Things* captures childhood in all its naughtiness, its shapeless fears, its nameless anxieties, it has been made possible by its language only. Chacko's 'infinite joy' is caught by the children in its phonetical aspect and becomes 'Infinnate Joy', Okay then becomes Okaythen, history becomes histry, Fine, thank you is compounded into Finethankyou. The Parade like walk of Sophie Mol is 'lef, lef, lefrightlef.' Later has been spelt as Lay Ter.

Sometimes phonetic sounds are used in order to highlight the important points or to bring out the strange impact of pronunciation. Lenin, the novice son of the anglophile K.N.M. Pillai, is made to recite Sir Walter Scott's 'Lochinvar' and the result is as hilarious as can be :

> O, young, Locin Varhas scum out of the vest,
> Through wall the vide Borer his teed was the bes;
> Tand savissgood broadsod heweapon sadnum,
> Nhe rod all unarmed, and he rod all lalone. (271)

Antony's speech — 'Lend me your ears' becomes, 'Lend me yaw years.' (274)

One word sentences abound and so do one-line paragraphs. But nowhere do they give a feeling that they are the result of the novelists strained effort to sound singular and unique. They come naturally and Roy makes sure they come inevitably. Roy seems to defy the laws of syntax. All her (grammatically) incomplete sentences convey sense so smoothly as no complete sentence in their place could ever do :

> Kochu Maria watched with her cakecrumb.
> The Fond Smiles watched Fondly.
> Little Girls playing.
> Sweet.
> One beach-coloured.

One brown.
One loved.
One Loved a Little less. (186)

One sentence paragraphs give the semblance of poetry in prose :

Who was he?
Who could he have been?
The God of Loss.
The God of Small Things.
The God of Gosse Bumps and Sudden
Smiles. (330)

This is sheer Poetry. *The Golden-Gate* is professedly a novel in verse, but if one were to name a contemporary prose novel in poetry, one could choose none but *The God of Small Things.* Like a sculptor, Roy cuts and polishes words, makes new, moulds new out of old ones and compounds new words by hyphenating them. Language is not allowed to pose barrier between Roy and her readers. She would tell them precisely what she wants to and not what words allow her to. If Velutha's unripeness and inexperience is to be conveyed, Roy uses youngness when even 'Youth' does not prove an apt choice.

Words beat at meanings like hammers, in her one word sentences producing staccato effect :

> He stroked her back. Very gently. She could feel the skin on his palms. Rough. Calloused. Sandpaper. (335)

Rahel's reminiscences about her maternal grandfather tell us about his strict rather inhuman attitude. He happened to be an entomologist who discovered a moth but could not get the credit for it. This left him bitter and frustrated. Since then the blame for all his outbursts goes to Pappachi's moth. It becomes associated with fear and terror. When Rahel notices Velutha holding a banner in the communist procession and says so openly. Ammu does not like it and looks threateningly at her. The hard look of anger in her face brings the memory of Pappachi's moth to her mind, 'How Pappachi's moth whispered in his children's veins' (72). When the terror strikes, the moth again sits on the children's chest, 'Inside the inspector's room, Pappachi's Moth was on the move' (316). In the darkness of night, Rahel and Estha search for Sophie Mol in the Meenachal river. They keep calling out, but no response. It seems she is drowned. 'On Rahel's heart Pappachi's moth snapped open its sombre wings.' (293)

The God of Small Things has a strong feminist perspective as well. The story of Pappachi's tormenting ways towards Mammachi is never forgotten by Ammu. Her own marital experience being equally bitter, she feels that all marriages are traps where the male has all rights to exercise power over the female and the lot of female is to suffer the agony of suppression. Again a metaphor describes the inequality of sexes quite brilliantly :

> As a child, she had learned very quickly to disregard the Father Bear Mother Bear stories she was given to read. In her version, Father Bear beat Mother Bear with brass vases. Mother Bear suffered those beatings with mute resignation. (180)

Some of Roy's sentences read like lines from T.S. Eliot :

> A tail, a tank, a wing.
> A wounded Machine.
> Melted Chocolates. Cigarette Sweets.
> Orangedrinks.
> Lemondrinks.
> CocaCola Fantaicecreamrosemilk.
> Pink-skinned dolls. Rattles. Love-in-Tokyos.
> Hollow plastic parakeets full of sweets with heads you could unscrew.
> Yellow-rimmed red sunglasses.
> Toy watches with the time painted on them.
> A cartful of defective toothbrushes.
> The Cochin Harbour Terminus. (301)

These are not sentences but sentence rhythms, which not only convey the author's intent but also create the desired effect.

V

If Roy has become an established writer by dint of this one novel only, the credit goes in a large measure, to her deft use of words which help create the desired ambience. Her store seems to be full of fresh, oven-hot words, 'Bluegreyblue,' (147), 'A Far More Angry Than Necessary feeling' (145). The week before Sophie Mol's arrival is marked by preparations and it is called, 'What will Sophie Mol Think week' (136). Divorced becomes Die-vorced, which is closer in meaning to its social implications. Natural and inanimate objects acquire character in the hands of Roy. Meenachal river is a powerful presence. It is one of the antagonists inasmuch as it becomes the medium for the oppressors to reach to Velutha. It is again one of the protagonists as it stands witness to the love of Velutha and Ammu as well as to the child-like adventures of the twins. Kari Saipu's house is 'History house' and the thick forest around it is 'heart of darkness.' It's not only because of the sunless thickness that it is dark but also because it is absolutely devoid of sympathy and pity, the milk of human kindness — to borrow from Shakespeare. It devours whatever comes to it, it finishes and crushes everything. At one place the reader comes across, 'Dark of Heartness tiptoed into the heart of Darkness' (306). Both these adjectives are highly significant. While heart of darkness is the central core of evil, dark of heartness is the dark recess of human heart, the devil in man. Both ways it is evil that it signifies.

Estha and Rahel have the habit of reading words in reverse order — Stop is read as Pots, welcome becomes emocleW, Spice is ecips. This habit accounts for much fun on the part of the children and quite a lot of annoyance to Miss Mitten — their private tutor — who takes it as an offence. They discover that madam and malayalam are palindromes. When the terror strikes and the children get to see the real face of police, Estha and Rahel sitting in the police station read the board on the wall in reverse order :

> EssenetitoP, Estha said. 'essenetiloP, ecneidebO,
> YtlayoL, ecnegilletnI, Rahel said.

> YsetruoC.
> YcneiciffE. (313)

This time, however it becomes symbolic as politeness, obedience, loyalty, intelligence, courtesy and efficiency — the self-proclaimed virtues of the police seem to have been thrown upside down by the inhuman behaviour of inspector Thomas Mathew.

Experimentation seems to be Roy's strong point and she makes full use of it. 'Locus Standi' is a term which the children overhear and its full implications not known, they take it as 'Locusts Stand I'. This, however suggests a new meaning and imparts new dimensions to the word. It suggests : 'I stand surrounded by Locusts' which creates an image of confusion that is created in Ammu's life when she is deprived of Locus Standi.

'Images lend vividness — a life like quality to writing' (1966) write Altenbernd and Lewis. Roy seems quite clever at painting images. Some lovely examples may be seen :

> Dead fish floated up in Estha. (320)
> One small life. A brief sunbeam. (293)
> Hairy fairies with lethal wands. (306)
> A brown leaf on his black back. That made the monsoons come on time. (294)

Though Roy claims that she wrote the book just as it came to her, and never had to rewrite a word of it, the novel as it is, seems to be a finished, polished specimen of language. One may also agree that it is her spontaneity that has lent this extraordinary charm to her language. It is through these that Roy creates another world and not only creates it, she pulls the reader into it, makes him the native of this world and forces him to remain in it for a long time to come. Long after one has finished reading the novel, the impact of that world is not lost. One can not shake off this world before long and all this has been made possible by words only. Roy creates ambience by the deft handling of words and proves her mettle as a writer of substance beyond doubt.

WORKS CITED

Altenbernd, Lynne and L. Lewis, Leslie, 1966. *A Handbook for The Study of Fiction.* New York : Macmillan.

Prabhu, Louella Lobo, "*The God of Small Things* — In Perspective". *Indian Book Chronicle*, Dec. 1997, p. 12.

Roy, Arundhati, 1997. *The God of Small Things.* New Delhi : IndiaInk.

17

Tughlaq as an Experimenter

—*Basavaraj Naikar*

GIRISH KARNAD'S *Tughlaq* depicts the life of the eponymous hero in relation to his subjects in his kingdom. It is true that he is a very wise man whose way of thinking appears to be foolish to the average man. The problems in Tughlaq's kingdom are caused as much by the peculiarities of his personality as by the unusualness of circumstances involving two contradictory cultures or religions. There are, therefore, two kinds of conflict affecting each other adversely.

The internal conflict may be seen between Tughlaq the clever administrator and Tughlaq the philosopher-poet. Tughlaq, for example, is an idealist who is influenced by the Greek philosophers like Plato and Socrates and therefore wants to achieve a balance between opposite principles. Besides, he suffers from the delusion of grandeur and acts the role of a god like Lord Krishna or that of a prophet like Jesus, without unfortunately having the omniscience or omnipotence of God. It is indeed paradoxical that he has not been able to achieve a balance within himself between his dream and his practical duty as an administrator, although he tomtoms about his desire to bring about a balance in all the walks of life. Most of the problems encountered by Tughlaq are the result of his inability to reconcile the opposite poles of dream and reality.

Had the population of his kingdom been of a homogeneous culture, Tughlaq would, perhaps, not have faced as many difficulties as he does now. The vertical schism in his self is unfortunately crossed and therefore worsened by the horizontal schism in the population of his kingdom itself. Tughlaq, for instance, would have fewer problems had the population of his kingdom been made up of only Muslims or only Hindus. But the exigencies of his life are such that he has to rule over a society which contains bi-cultural values, attitudes and expectations. What is most conspicuous about such a heterogeneous society is that one culture is diametrically opposed to the other (in this case, Hinduism is pitted against Islam) in many a detail. It is the antagonistic nature of these two major cultures (or religions) that makes the Sultan suffer alternately at the hands of Hindus and Muslims. Tughlaq's foolishness lies precisely in his attempt to achieve a balance between these irreconcilable cultures. Hence the external conflict between the protagonist and the antagonist *i.e.* the population of his kingdom as a whole.

A few details of the external conflict between the Sultan and his people are necessary to show how he suffers continuously at the hands of people belonging to mutually exclusive cultures. Although the idealistic emperor wants to achieve a balance between Hindus and Muslims, he fails to realize that it is not wanted by his own co-religionists. The Muslims of his kingdom, for instance, are fundamentalists who do not like the Hindus being exempted from the payment of *jiziya* tax. Further, they do not like the emperor showing special kindness and concessions to the Hindus. (In this case Tughlaq looks like Mahatma Gandhi who fought for the Hindu-Muslim unity in modern India.) But when the emperor continues to maintain an image of impartiality for himself, the Muslims would like to exploit the opportunity by trapping him in his own virtue. Aziz is an incarnation of this exploitatory mischief. He takes the guise of a *brahmin* called Vishnu Prasad and wins a case against the Sultan himself thereby achieving two things simultaneously *i.e.* getting a personal profit at the Sultan's cost and giving the Sultan a sense of satisfaction of being lenient towards Hindus. Similarly the Sultan's decision to transfer the Kingdom from Delhi to Daulatabad is motivated by his desire to bring about a balance between the Delhi-based Muslims and the Daulatabad-based Hindus and is therefore strongly resented by the Muslims.

That the Sultan is a clever administrator is indubitable indeed. He knows the art of projecting an image of impartial figure to the public. He wants not only to be good to the people, but also to be widely to be good to them. That is the reason why he orders his announcers to declare to the people how Vishnu Prasad, a brahmin from Bikaner won a suit against himself (Sultan). Likewise he has invited the holy man Shaikh Imamuddin and allowed him to criticise himself (Sultan) publicly. He is so clever that he traps the Shaikh himself in his fundamentalism and succeeds in persuading him to act as his royal envoy to Ainul Mulk. The Sultan has made prayer compulsory in his kingdom, but when the Muslim amirs try to murder him at prayer time, he cancels prayers in his kingdom until Abbasid Khalif comes to Daulatabad and starts it once again. The Sultan who asked Shihabuddin to take care of his kingdom in his absence, does not hesitate to stab him to death when he discovers that the latter had conspired against him. Later when Aziz impersonates the holy man Abbasid Khalif after murdering the latter, the Sultan is smart enough to expose him, but yet like a director of drama, orders him to playact the role of the holy man before the public and start the prayers. Likewise, he prescribes death by stone-pelting to his stepmother who has had Najib murdered. In all these situations, the Sultan acts very quickly like an able administrator and resembles Macbeth. He never Hamletizes over any situation.

But the clever administrator in Tughlaq is not reconciled to the poet-philosopher in him. The two talents in him remain absurdly apart. His desire to indulge in the study of heavenly stars and great poetry has, perhaps, made him blind to the human nature. Although he tries to create a balance between Hindus and Muslims, it never occurs to him that a Muslim like Aziz could deceive him mischievously and hypocritically. His desire to introduce copper currency on par with silver dinars is, of course, evidence of advanced economic arrangement. But the fault lies in his inability to see the possibility of misuse of the new currency. Nor has he taken precaution to prevent such curruption in the kingdom. Aziz and Azam, therefore, take advantage of the situation to paralyse the economic order. History, thus, goes out of the Sultan's control thereby making him aware of his follies. He learns a belated lesson of his life. His impractical idealism is defeated by the ugly reality. But the defeat of Tughlaq or his idealism does not raise him to that height of a tragic hero, as it does not involve any self-sacrifice (unlike the other tragic figures like Macbeth or Agamemnon). One reason for this could, perhaps, be that he never had a selfish motive in his desire to convert his kingdom into a Utopia. One may easily describe him as an experimentalist who revises his philosophy, however idealistic it may be, in the light of the practical knowledge of reality. When he realises his folly, he has the open-mindedness to transfer his capital back from Daulatabad to Delhi without having any sense of shame or humiliation. That several families were sacrificed in the process of this experimentation is, perhaps, inevitable. It is, therefore, not proper for us to describe him as a tragic hero. In spite of his absurd behaviour, he has the liberal attitude towards life which enables him to give up the *a priori* knowledge in favour of *a posteriori* one. He has nothing to lose personally as he has nothing to gain either. The internal conflict is resolved finally when his addiction to stars is cured by the practical administrative alertness. Similarly the external conflict between the Sultan and the population of the Kingdom is resolved when the latter are defeated by him thereby awakening his sense of reality. It is, therefore, better to call Tughlaq an experimenter than a tragic hero. As the population of his kingdom, however large in quantity, is not equal to him in power and therefore becomes an easy victim for his political experimentation.

WORK CITED

Girish Karnad, *Tughlaq*, Delhi Oxford University Press, 1986.

18

The Use of Myth in Girish Karnad's *The Fire and the Rain*

—*Mukesh Ranjan Verma*

ONE OF the greatest tasks before writers has been to find an adequate mode to communicate the incommunicable. In their search for, to use T.S. Eliot's famour phrase, an 'objective correlative' to emotions, feelings and thoughts, the writers have found myth a very effective mode. In these traditional accounts of the exploits of national or cultural heroes, both mortal and immortal the writers have found a reference point, an archetype, a parallel or even a contrast to be used for saying what they want to say. Hazel E. Barnes has remarked in his *Myth and Human Experience* :

> "In a period when values are relatively stable, authors tend to use the classical myths merely allusively, enriching the poetic quality of their work with layers of older connotations. In an age more obviously transitional there is likely to be more of new interpretations."[1]

It is in the latter context that the use of myth in the plays of Girish Karnad acquires significance. Among the modern Indian writers, Girish Karnad has been the foremost to make a very expressive use of myth in his plays. While writing his very first play, *Yayati*, he found the story of king Yayati from the *Mahabharata* providing a very powerful emotional equivalent to what he wanted to communicate. He writes in the introduction to his *Three Plays* :

> "The myth had enabled me to articulate to myself a set of values that I had been unable to arrive at rationally."[2]

In his play, *The Fire and the Rain* which was first staged in Minneapolis, USA in 1994, and was published in 1998, and which is the English translation of his Kannada play, *Agni Mattu Male* by the writer himself, Karnad turns once again to myth to present a moving tale of love, jealousy and loneliness. The action of the play is centred around a seven-year long fire sacrifice conducted to propitiate the rain god, Indra, to end a devastating spell of drought. In this background is woven a complex story of hurt egos, awe-inspiring spiritual powers that are harnessed only to serve jealous ends, and all encompassing love which raises a man above the plane of a mere mortal. It is through a relatively less known myth of Yavakri and Paravasu from the *Mahabharata* that Karnad has been able to give a force and universality to some of the basic human passions.

The myth of Yavakri and Paravasu occurs in chapters 135-38 in the "Vana Parva" of the *Mahabharata*. It is narrated by the ascetic Lomasha to Yudhistir, the Pandava prince, when the Pandavas were wandering across the land during their exile. It is the story of two sages, Bharadwaja and Raibhya and their sons. Though both the sages were very learned and endowed with spiritual powers, it was Raibhya who was appointed the royal priest. His sons, Paravasu and Aravasu, were also learned priests. Bharadwaja's son, Yavakri or Yavakrit nursed a grievance against the world, particularly against Raibhya and his sons, for he felt that his father had not been accorded the recognition that he deserved. So he went into the forest to do a rigorous penance to please the king of gods, Indra. After some years, moved by the rigour of his penance, Indra appeared before him. Yavakri requested him to grant him the knowledge of the Vedas. Indra, however, told him that knowledge could only be gained over the years from a 'guru'. He asked Yavakri to go back, but he was not willing to listen to him. He continued with his 'tapasya'. This forced Indra to ultimately grant him his wish.

When Yavakri came back, proud of his achievement, Bharadwaja warned him against delusions of omnipotence. He particularly asked him not to meddle with Raibhya who was known for his anger. His fears however, proved true as Yavakri one day cornered Raibhya's daughter-in-law and forced her to have sex with him. When Raibhya came to know of it, he was so incensed that he invoked the 'Kritya' spirit. By making oblations of the strands of his hair he invoked two spirits — one a 'rakshasa' and another a look-alike of his daughter-in-law, and sent them to kill Yavakri. While Yavakri was having his mid-day meal, the female spirit went to him and stole his pot of consecrated water. The 'rakshasa' then pursued him. Yavakri needed water to invoke his powers, but every spot with a bit of water dried up at his approach. Finally, he tried to enter his father's hermitage, but the blind man who guarded his father's hermitage blocked his entry. The rakshasa who was behind him killed him with a trident.

Though Bharadwaja knew that Yavakri had been punished for his misdeed, his grief made him impervious to reason. He cursed Raibhya that he would be killed by his own son. And shocked at the folly of what he had done, he immolated himself. Raibhya's sons — Paravasu and Aravasu — were conducting a fire sacrifice for the king. One night Paravasu came to his cottage. He mistook his father, who was wearing a deerskin, for a wild animal and shot him dead with his arrow. When he realized what he had done, he cremated his father and returned to his sacrificial enclosure. There he told his brother about their father's death and asked him to go and perform the penitential rites prescribed for Brahminicide since he could not carry on the fire sacrifice alone. Meanwhile he would conduct the sacrifice. Aravasu did his brother's bidding. But when he returned to the sacrifice, Paravasu told the king that he should not be allowed to enter the sacrificial enclosure as he was a Brahmin-killer.

A stunned Aravasu loudly protested that this was a lie and that Paravasu himself had killed his father, but nobody listened to him. He was thrown out by the King's guards. Aravasu retired to the jungle and prayed to the sun god for help. The sun god obliged him. It became known to the king that Aravasu was innocent and it was Paravasu who had killed his father. The King ordered Paravasu to go away, and invited Aravasu to conduct the fire sacrifice. Later on, the sun god restored Yavakri, Bharadwaja and Raibhya back to life at the request of Aravasu and made Paravasu forget his evil act. When Yavakri came back to life, he was reprimanded by gods for his folly and asked to pursue knowledge in the right spirit.

Girish Karnad, as he tells us in the preface to the play, had come across this myth in C. Rajagopalachari's abridgment of the *Mahabharata*, while he was still in college. He was fascinated, by it and the myth continued to return to him, but it took him more than three decades to turn it into a play. He writes :

> "For the next thirty-seven years, I struggled with it, trying to fit all the ramifications of the myth within some sort of manageable shape."[3]

And, as he himself tells in his Notes to the play, "Thirty-seven years is a long time to live with a myth for a company. It inevitably grows and changes with one."[4] Karnad's story certainly differs from the original myth in some important regards. Unlike the myth, Bhardwaja and Raibhya in Karnad's story are not just friends but brothers, and so their children are cousins. Karnad makes Yavakri and Vishakha, Raibhya's daughter-in-law, lovers and thus gives a new twist to the story. In the myth, Raibhya creates a look-alike of his daughter-in-law and sends her to facilitate the killing of Yavakri. In the play, Vishakha goes to Yavakri to warn him against the Brahma Rakshasa whom her father-in-law has sent to kill him. She does deprive Yavakri of his consecrated water, but the situation this time is different. Raibhya as conceived by Karnad in the play, is entirely different from the Raibhya of the myth. In the myth Paravasu kills his father inadvertently, but in the play he does so deliberately. In the myth, the Brahma Rakshasa, after killing Yavakri goes to live with the female spirit created by Raibhya. But in the play, he seeks liberation from his state of limbo between life and death. This gives a new dimension to the play. The greatest change that Karnad has brought about in the myth is in the character of Aravasu (pronounced in the play as

'Arvasu'). Unlike the myth, Arvasu of the play is not a learned priest. On the other hand, he is a young man of 18 who loves dancing and acting in play, something which was prohibited for Brahmins. Not only that, he is madly in love with a tribal girl, Nittilai and is keen on marrying her. Nittilai is a creation of Karnad, and through the love of Arvasu and Nittilai he has given an altogether new meaning to the myth. A significant addition to the myth in the play is the story of Indra and Vritra presented through the playlet enacted by the troupe of actors and Arvasu to entertain the priests at the fire sacrifice.

The slaying of the demon, Vritra, by Indra is one of the archetypal myths of India which appeared for the first time in the *Rigveda* and much later with variations in the *Mahabharata*. It is the Mahabharata version of the myth that Karnad uses in the play. In this version Indra, Vritra and Vishwarupa are brothers — all sons of Brama. Indra feels threatened by the popularity of Vishwarupa and kills him treacherously, while Vritra tries in vain to save him. Karnad's incorporation of the Indra-Vritra myth in the play reinforces one of the central themes of *The Fire and the Rain* — The treachery of a brother against another. Karnad says about it :

> "The myth can be seen as expressing a deep anxiety which informs the whole of Indian mythology, the fear of brother destroying brother. This fear branches out fully and nakedly in the *Mahabharata*, where the bonding of brothers within the Pandava and the Kuru clans is as close as the enmity between the cousins is ruthless and unrelenting. In the *Ramayana*, the fraternal bonding in the Raghu family — Rama and his brothers — expresses another facet of the same anxiety with the betrayals of Sugriva and Vibhishana (interestingly in the cause of the ethically correct side) marking the counterpoint.
>
> The tale of Aravasu and Paravasu fascinated me as unusual variant of this Indian obsession with fratricide and it seemed logical too that Yavakri should be their cousin, though the *Mahabharata* does not explicitly say so, I cannot remember when I decided to incorporate the

> Indra-Vritra legend in my plot, but years later, while re-reading the original version, I was astonished to find that right at the beginning of the tale of Yavakri, Lomasha mentions that the whole story took place on the banks of a river in which Indra had bathed to cleanse himself of the sin of killing Vritra! One of the fascinating aspects of dealing with the myths is their self-reflexivity. A myth seems complete in itself and yet when examined in detail contains subconscious signals which lead you on to another myth which in turn will act as a conduit to a third one while illuminating the one you started with."[5]

The brother-hatred theme in *The Fire and the Rain* is incorporated in Yavakri-Paravasu conflict though Paravasu is not directly involved in the conflict and Yavakri meets his end not through Paravasu but Raibhya. Karnad shifts the focus of the conflict from the first generation — that of Bharadwaja and Raibhya —, to the second generation — that of their sons — by removing Bharadwaja from the scene. In the play, when Yavakri returns from his ten year long 'tapasya', Bharadwaja is already dead, having died of a broken heart at the foolish pursuit of his son. Whatever Yavakri does is a calculated move to incite Paravasu. He is burning with a desire to humiliate Paravasu and his family. He says to Vishakha :

> "Grievances! you don't even flatter me with the word 'hatred'. But it doesn't matter. What matters is that I hate your husband's family. My father deserved to be invited as the Chief Priest of the sacrifice. But that too went to Paravasu, your husband. Even in the midst of my austerities I wept when I heard the news. For I knew father would refuse to take offence. I knew he would go and congratulate Paravasu on the honour, embrace and bless him."[6]

So he fixes everything — his meeting with Vishakha and his sexual act with her. He tells her later that if she had not agreed to it of her own accord, he would have taken her by force. So that this becomes known to all, he calls Raibhya back a day earlier than his scheduled return. He even fixes the timing of his deed and asks Aravasu to meet him specifically at that time. He is rather waiting for the challenge from the other side so that he could prove his might by frustrating their challenge. It is Raibhya, and not Paravasu, who picks up the challenge and destroys him.

Karnad has presented Paravasu as the symbol of supreme egotism who is trying through the fire sacrifice not to seek blessings from Indra but to equal him. He regards Yavakri beneath contempt. He says to Vishakha :

> "One can practice austerities like your fool, Yavakri, to coerce the gods to bend to one's will. Stand in a circle of fire. Torture oneself. So many techniques, all equally crass to make the gods appear. And when they give in what do you do? Extend the begging bowl : 'Give us rains. Cattle. Sons. Wealth. As though one defined human beings by their begging — I despise it. I went because the fire sacrifice is a formal rite. Structured. It involves no emotional acrobatics from the participants. The process itself will bring Indra to me, and if anything goes wrong, there's nothing the gods can do about it. It has to be set right by a man. By me. That's why when the moment comes I shall confront Indra in silence. As an equal. For that it is essential that one shed all human weakness. Be alone. Absolutely on ones' own to face that moment. Become a diamond. Unscratchable."[7]

The speech provides us an insight into Paravasu's character as it also provides us a clue to his killing of his father as well as his treachery towards his younger brother. In the myth Paravasu kills his father by mistake, under the curse of Bharadwaja. In the play, he does so intentionally. Just before he kills him, Vishakha has been accusing her father-in-law of sexually abusing her. So she thinks that Paravasu has killed him because of this accusation and tells him that now he will never know whether she told him a lie. In response Paravasu tells her :

> "You didn't need to. He deserved to die. He killed Yavakri to disturb me in the last stages of the sacrifice.

> Not to punish Yavakri but to be even with me. I had to attend to him before he went any farther."[8]

He could not allow anyone to disturb the fire sacrifice which was nearing completion, and herein lies the reason of his betrayal of his younger brother who doted on him and who followed blindly whatever he told him. Aravasu is baffled at Paravasu's behaviour and so the only thing that he keeps shouting in the sacrificial enclosure when Paravasu accuses him of patricide and he is being thrown out by the guards is — "But why, Bother, why? why? why? Tell me why, please."[9]

In his effort to 'shed all human weakness' and to become 'a diamond, Unscratchable', Paravasu loses all human sentiments — sentiments that make human beings, so vulnerable yet so lovable. The Brahma Rakshasa approaches him, begging him to help him in getting liberation from his limbo. He claims that since Raibhya had created him, he is his brother, but Paravasu is simply not interested. He says to him that he does not need any more bother.

What Paravasu lacks, Aravasu has full to the brim — a zest for life and a love for others. At the end of the play, it is for him that Indra appears. He tells him to ask to anything he wants. People urge Aravasu to ask for rain, Brahma Rakshasa implores him to ask for his liberation, he himself wants his Nittilai back to life. But when Brahma Rakshasa tells him that his Nittilai would not like life at the cost of some one suffering eternally, Aravasu is moved. He asks Indra to grant Brahma Rakshasa his release. This noble gesture ultimately brings rain to the parched land.

It is this interpretation of the myth that knowledge without love, compassion, understanding and humanity can only lead to inflated egos, jealous hearts and finally all-round destruction that makes *The Fire and the Rain* so moving a play.

REFERENCES

1. Hazel, E. Barnes, quoted by A.S. Phand, *Essays on Comparative Literature* (New Delhi : Sterling Publisher, 1984), p. 110.
2. Girish Karnad, Introduction to *Three Plays* (Delhi : Oxford University Press, 1998).

3. Girish Karnad, Preface to *The Fire and the Rain* (Delhi : Oxford University Press, 1998).
4. *The Fire and Rain*, p. 74.
5. *Ibid.*, pp. 68-69.
6. *Ibid.*, p. 22
7. *Ibid.*, pp. 31-32
8. *Ibid.*, p. 33.
9. *Ibid.*, p. 38.

19

A Closer Look at the Hidden Psyche of Jayanta Mahapatra

—M.A. Nare

JAYANTA MAHAPATRA is now a major Indian poet writing in English. He was the first to win The National 'Sahitya Akademy' Award for Poetry for the book *'Relationshp'* in 1981. Then followed the poets, Nissim Ezekiel, Kamala Das and Shiv K. Kumar.

In this critical paper I would like to reveal some of the hidden layers of the psyche of this great poet from Orissa (India).

Jayanta Mahapatra, educated at a Missionary school, under British, Australian and Anglo-Indian teachers was a Reader in Physics, at Ravenshaw College, Cuttack-Orissa.

About his knowledge of English Literature and composition of a poem in English, he writes :

> "More than twenty years ago, when I first started writing poetry I decided to test my powers at poetry by sending the poems out to various periodicals. At that time frankly, I knew very little about poetry, my knowledge of the subject being limited to a few poems of Keats, Shelley and Wordsworth that had been incorporated in our school literature texts. To me this was a severe test, because the act of writing a poem was totally unknown to me."
>
> "My efforts were in all probability directed towards something new, a 'modernity' in my poetry. Undeniably I did want to write poems that would be different from those that still stuck to my mind from my school days. On the other hand, my ideas of what would be called

> 'modern' in the realm of poetry were vague. Nor did I have any access to contemporary poetry then."[1]

Thus he gives a detailed account of his early poetic career in his paper presented at the Seminar on — "Indian Literature : An End-Century Assessment" organised by the Sahitya Akademy at New Delhi — during 20-24 February 1991.[2]

'*Chandrabhaga*' the literary Journal he edited from Cuttack-Orissa (India) helped him as the Ambassador-at-large of his poetry to America, England and other countries. Thus, he could establish his relationship with American and English poets, editors, critics and readers. It seems, for a long time, Indian editors, poets, critics and readers found it difficult to understand his poetry.

So, he began to send his poems to American and English periodicals and they were regularly published in the following Journals and magazines '*Chicago Review*', *Poetry*, '*Sewanee Review*', '*Critical Quarterly*', '*Malahat Review*', '*Times Literary Supplement*' and *Queen's Quarterly*.

In 1975 he won Poetry's Jacob Glastein Memorial Award. But from the publication of his great poem 'Relationship' in 1980 by The Greenfield Review Press, New York (U.S.A.) he drew attention of the people, who ultimately recommended it for The National 'Sahitya Akademy' Award for Poetry.

The Sahitya Akademy Award for his book 'Relationship' inspired many Indian and foreign critics to write assessments of his poetry in general and '*Relationship*' in particular.

But no one has so far focused his/her attention on the hidden struggle of his Christian psyche, its deep-rooted agony and the problem of alienation which stood before him like the historic Berlin wall that kept him away from the people of his own motherland Orissa and its Ancient Cultural Heritage so dear to his heart.

His wounded Christian psyche lay dormant like a volcano only to erupt at a later stage in his poetic career. Through this eruption, a new Jayanta Mahapatra was born and we can see the struggle of his psyche in the two poems 'Myth' and 'Grandfather'.

Let us see how his Christian psyche received a terrible blow of humiliation on one occasion when he tried to enter the famous Hindu Temple with a genuine desire to worship the deity. (Myth)

This incident symbolically reveals the great humiliations he must have experienced in his life. The poem reveals only the tip of the iceburg of the agony, humiliation, anger, anguish, frustration, a feeling of rootlessness in his own land — a feeling that finally turns his mind to the past and reveals to him the sacrifices made by his brown ancestors, nameless as stones.

All his racial consciousness culminated in the composition of his great poem : '*Relationship*'. This touching incident is dramatically presented in his poem — Myth.

"The stairs seem endless,
life long,
and those peaks too, Annapurna,
Dhaulgiri,
Uncertain, impressive as gods,
I dare not go
into the dark, dark sanctum
where the myth shifts
swiftly from hand to hand,
eye to eye.

The dried, sacrificed flowers smile at me.
I have become;
a diamond in the eye.
Vague grieving years pit against distant peaks
like a dying butterfly
as a bearded, saffron-robed man
asks me, firmly :
Are you a Hindoo?"[3]

What a terrible blow it must have been to the wounded psyche of this sensitive poet.

The image of the dying butterfly is highly suggestive.

The winged-psyche suffered a terrible blow and through its death throes a new psyche was born.

He must have remained satisfied with an illusion that the Glory of Orissa's Cultural Heritage belonged to him as much as it belonged to any other person in Orissa.

But 'The saffron-robed bearded Hindoo' Priest gave his psyche a death blow.

And from this moment he began to ask his motherland Orissa *i.e.*, 'Kalinga' a pertinent question — Who am I ?

'On his own Muse Mahapatra writes :

> 'These poems are just attempts of mine to hold a handful of earth to my face and let it speak — perhaps this signifies to my roots so that they reveal Who I am?'[4]

So, he turned to his dead grandfather to know why he had embraced Christianity. For many years he must have felt that his grandfather had committed a grave mistake in embracing Christianity and leaving his Ancestral Religion and its Heritage.

It seems, he took three years to complete this poem. It reveals the struggle of his wounded psyche to come out of its cocoon. Beneath the title *'Grandfather'* these words appear :

(Starving on the point of death, Chintamani Mahapatra embraced Christianity during the terrible famine that struck Orissa in 1866.)

The poem begins with these words :

'The yellowed pages of his diary's notes whisper in vernacular'. Through those pages his grandfather's invisible presence haunts him like 'The Ghost of Hamlet's father and forces him to hear that voice.' Jayanta Mahapatra seems to have grasped the intensity and the dimensions of the terrible crisis faced by his grandfather. So he writes :

> "For you it was the hardest Question of all
> Dead, empty trees stood by the
> dragging river,
> past your weakened body,
> flailing against your sleep

you thought of the way the jakals
moved, to move.
Did you hear the young tamarind leaves rustle
in the cold mean nights of your belly ?
Did you see your own death?
Watch it tear at your cries?"[5]

As you read this poem you easily realise a kind of shift in his attitude to his Grandfather like the shift in "W.B. Yeats' attitude to the Irish Rebels in the poem, 'Easter 1916'."

He raises the rhetorical questions :

"What did faith matter ?
What Hindu world so ancient and
true for you to hold?
The separate life let you survive
While perhaps
The one you left wept in the
Blurb of your heart."[6]
"Grandfather you are an invisible
piece on a board
whose move has made our children
grow, to know us,
Carrying us deep where our voices
lapse into silence.
We wish to know you more
We wish we knew what it was
to be against dying,
to know the dignity
That had to be earned dangerously."[7]

So the shift is quite clear now, he is on the side of his Grandfather and the poor nameless ancestors who fought bravely to defend his ancient kingdom 'Kalinga'.

The ten thousand soldiers who were massacred in the battle of Kalinga : (B.C. 261) by the great army of Ashoka, the ruthless invader, were his ancestors.

He also pleads the case of the nameless warriors, shipmen who sacrificed their lives in guarding the coast from Chilka to Chandipur. 'Kalinga was a great maritime nation in the olden days', he writes in the notes.

Many readers fail to understand that he is not on the side of Ashoka the Great 'Who erected peace edicts on 'blood red rocks' but he is pleading the case of the brave, Oriya soldiers massacred at Dhauli on the bank of the river Daya.

Their blood flowed through the river Daya, and their corpses were scattered on the battlefield to be torn by wolves, jakals and vultures.

While talking about the artisans of stones, his other ancestors who built the great temples like the sun temple at Konark (Orissa), Mahapatra writes in his *Relationship* :

> "We have come as dreams
> disguised that pinned us down,
> artisans of stone,
> messengers of spirit
> twelve hundred artless brown
> flowers in passion
> to the night in humble brother-hood
> aerial roots of a centuries old banyan tree;
> not taking life seriously
> for our lives are only of the seeds of dreams,
> forgetting the cruelties
> of ruthless emperors who
> carved peaceful edicts
> on blood red Rock
> forgetting our groans, and cries,
> the smells of gunsmoke and smouldering flesh."[8]

In section three of the *'Relationship'* the poet shows how ruthlessly Ashoka invaded his ancient kingdom Kalinga and then seeing the great massacre felt a change of heart :

> "It is hard to tell now what opened the anxious skies,
> how the age old proud stones
> lost their strength and fell,
> how the waters of Daya
> stank with the bodies of my ancestors;
> my eyes close now,
> because of the fear that moves my skin :
> the invaders walk along the only

road they know
That leads to their bloody victories."[9]

And that is why, Jayanta Mahapatra while accepting the 'Sahitya Akademy Award' spoke these words :

"To Orissa, to this land in which my roots lie and lies my past and in which lie my beginning and end — I acknowledge my debt and relationship."[10]

'*Relationship*' reveals Jayanta Mahapatra's great efforts to transform his 'mute inglorious' sufferings which he connects with the sufferings of his nameless ancestors whose great sacrifices made them 'the stones' — a symbol W.B. Yeats uses for the Irish Rebels who became national heroes — through their great sacrifice. (see Easter 1916)

'Many saffron-robed, bearded men will come and go — but the poetry of Jayanta Mahapatra will shine as long as men and women find time to read poetry of this Ancient Land and this will give a new life to his ancestors.'

Through his '*Relationship*' they shine like the innumerable stars in the Galaxy.

NOTES

1. *The Bombay Literary Review*, Published by University of Bombay, Number 1, 1991, pp. 5 to 6.
2. *Ibid.,* pp. 5 to 11.
3. Jayanta Mahapatra, *A Rain of'Rites,* University of Georgia Press, 1976, p. 22.
4. Madhusudan Prasad (ed.), *The Poetry of Jayanta Mahapatra : A Critical Study*, p. 171. Sterling Publishers Private Ltd., 1986.
5. Jayanta Mahapatra, *Life Signs* (Oxford University Press), 1983, p. 19.
6. *Ibid.,* p. 19
7. *Ibid*., p. 20.
8. Jayanta Mahapatra, *'Relationship'* First Indian Edition, 1982, Chandrabhaga Society, Cuttack (India), pp. 9-10.
9. *Ibid*., p. 14.
10. Madhusudan Prasad (ed.), *The Poetry of Jayanta Mahapatra : A Critical Study*, p. 156.

20

The Satirical Poetry of T.R. Rajasekharaiah

—Basavaraj Naikar

T.R. RAJASEKHARAIAH (1926 —) happens to be a late bloomer in Indian English poetry like Shiv K. Kumar. He had published his first collection of Kannada poems entitled *Rudraksi* as early as 1966 and earned the Karnataka State Sahitya Academy Award for it the next year. The poems in *Rudraksi* were cast in the romantic or *navodaya* mould. T.R. Rajasekharaiah was a Professor of English at Karnatak University, Dharwad and Chairman of the English Department at Gulbarga University, Gulbarga until his retirement in 1986. During 1964-66, he went to USA as a Fulbright Senior Visiting Professor and taught in Fairleigh Dickinson University, NJ, and State University of New York at Buffalo. He was also a Fellow of the University of Minnesota in 1964-65 and of New York University in 1965-66. An original thinker and an excellent orator, he addressed many clubs and cultural associations of America about Indian culture, literature and philosophy. He carried out his post-doctoral research work on Walt Whitman and published his famous *Roots of Whitman's Grass* from the Fairleigh Dickinson University Press. As he grew into a brilliant academician and studied American poetry deeply, his own poetic mode slowly changed from romantic to realistic, especially satirical one. After his return from America in 1966, he felt deeply depressed and disillusioned with the squalid life in India. Nauseated by the Indian filth, superstition and squalor, angered by the Indian communalism and hypocrisy and irritated by the

Indian callous bureaucracy, opportunistic politics and standardisation of corruption at all walks of life. T.R. Rajasekharaiah was compelled to resort to the writing of realistic and satirical poetry. Although he had been writing his poems from 1960s, he had not come out with any collection of poems. I, therefore, brought out a bulky collection of ninety and odd poems entitled *Desert Blooms* in 1986, on the eve of his retirement from Gulbarga University, Gulbarga.

On the whole T.R. Rajasekharaiah's poetry may be described as cerebral and easily invites comparison with similar poetry of Shiv K. Kumar, Jayanta Mahapatra and Nissim Ezekiel. His poetry may be sub-classified into four categories : one, philosophical; two, satirical; three, humorous and four, romantic. In the present article an attempt has been made to introduce some of his satirical poetry.

The deep sense of disillusionment felt by Rajasekharaiah about life in India has been expressed into titular poem "Desert Blooms" where the metaphor of desert dominates and easily brings to our mind Eliotian metaphor of the wasteland. The poet is conscious of the special strength of the human soul and will power to survive in the desert in spite of all the inconveniences and encumbrances. The horridness and the destructive aspect of the desert are expressed in the following lines :

Under the life-stifling layers of sand
That holds life in this my land
And here in this State, an arid part
Of a brazen continent and this shallow hole,
The vital sheets of unseen water, womb of life,
That God put beyond the drying power of man's error,
Yet stretch and flow and reach and suckle
And so flowers bloom in beds of sand.

The aridity of life caused by the desert is deeply felt by the poet who was condemned by the quirks of his fate to spend the latter part of his professional career in "an arid part of a brazen continent" *i.e.,* Gulbarga especially after having had the beautiful and memorable experiences in the green pastures of Bangalore,

Dharwad and America. Lack of aesthetic approach, inability to appreciate the intellectual achievements, commercialization of every problem, irrational communalism, opportunistic behaviour, lack of discrimination between Good and Bad, the beautiful and the ugly; the able and the inefficient etc., are some of the dominant features of Indian life microscopically symbolised by Gulbarga which compel the sensitive poet like Rajasekharaiah to be disillusioned with them.

The poet's disappointment with Indian life is satirically articulated in many poems. In "The Man Who Was Afraid," for example, he pinpoints the difficulty of living amidst multiple inconveniences, foolishnesses, inefficiencies and ironies in India. One has to live in India in perpetual fear and in an atmosphere of insecurity :

> It's fear : stark naked fear;
> Not of death that kills, nor of the punishing hell;
> Nor of a heaven cheated.
> This earth is our mind's bugbear,
> Fear of the thorny fence of our neighbour
> Bleeding our fruit. This is a land of unfixities.

The uncertainties of life happen to be man-made, but sometimes, unfortunately, raised to the pseudo-philosophical height of 'luck' or 'chance' :

> ...An element of luck, so much
> The ungodly, shapes portions of history
> Here. Air! Often you need a middleman,
> A special word of recommendation,
> To buy your package of cigarettes.
> Next minutes uncertainty tolls the bell
> All the time.

The uncertainty is caused by the absence of a common principle and lack of co-ordination between people and their egos. Each one seems to be a mini-Hitler not caring for the otherness of life :

> The bus driver to the housekeeper
> Clerk, labourer, officer,
> Each is the master of the land

Stretching around.
For each his bow, the fee,
The show of fealty.
Every step our feet tread
There is an office of dread.

What is most annoying is the legalisation (Shall I say sanctification or governmentalisation?) of inefficiency and the farcical acceptance of it as the elevated truth. This aspect of Indian life is bitterly and satirically attacked by the poet :

The flow of the river halts for the salaam,
The turnpike opens upon the due deposit,
The bad grammar of a police constable
Can stay the march of stars for a night at least,
For like the mule he bears the palanquin.

The satirical attack is very powerfully articulated in the "Theme of Sorrow." The poem is reflective in tone. It begins with a negative reference to Thomas Gray's elegy and later shows the contrast between India and the West. Far from being a matter of sorrow, death becomes a matter of relief and even jubilation and advertisement in India. The poet, obviously, shows the reversal of normality :

Elegies in this land
Are not to be written in the churchyard,
Country or own, upon the dead lowered
Into the earth.

After making a general satirical observation on India, the poet proceeds to show the reversal of values :

...Theirs is not the theme of sorrow.
The undoing that death does to them
Is almost a making, a thing to be
Devoutly desired and gladly thanked for
Much for that little relief.

After showing how death is a matter of relief rather than that of sorrow, he offers a few details of the death of human spirit in India in abstract words followed by a metaphor :

Here is death,
That emptiness, inanity, unbeing.

Words without meaning.
Action without intent
Motion without grace;
Living is enemy to life.

The abstract observation is followed by a concrete metaphor :

Living is enemy to life, the eerie lamps
By which limbs stir turning the bustle of energy
Into a witches' dance around the broomstick.

The images of witches' dance, eerie lamps and broomstick signify the dismal aspect of death as well as the entertainmental dimension associated with it.

The final part of the poem crystallises the theme of death in a beautiful metaphor of 'burnt piece of mutton.' He says :

The soul is a burnt piece of mutton, corroded
By all the fires of corrupt concepts,
Twisted ideals, degenerate though and feeling
But with dressing
The coffins sparkle in the jabbering parade,
Mocking death's dignity in masquerade.

The death of human spirit is articulated through the culinary image of a 'burnt piece of mutton' and becomes a subject not for sorrow but for parade and mockery. The poet's bitterness about and disapproval of the reversal of the normal values of life in India appear to be very genuine as they come from the bottom of his heart and incidentally remind us of Eliotian vision of the West as a wasteland proving a good parallel to India.

In "Valour" Rajasekharaiah expresses his bitterness about life in India which is marked by continuous sorrow and frustration. He reverses the common saying and declares that :

To die that once, honoured Shakespeare
Surely shouldn't need so much valour!

He recognizes the existential predicament of the modern Indian who is too helpless to rebel against the dire conditions around him :

Dawn to night and night to morning,
Month after month we have died
Ten thousand times.

The poet bitterly points out the overall corruption of the very atmosphere in which we are condemned to live :

The air we breathe, the fare we chew,
Even the anodynes for pain and woe
Have destroyed us hourly,
And our uninflammable spirit
Has burnt to drop the gall and raise from ashes.

But the continuous suffering of man at different phases of his life has paradoxically made him a hero. The poet compliments him for his courage to die so often in order to wade through his existence :

The coward dies just once in life,
We are the valiants, we who keep this strife.

Rajasekharaiah's pessimism and disappointment find expression in "Bitterness." He recounts how in spite of his ebulliant pride, he is reduced to the level of a weak man by the forces beyond his control. The Indian sun acts as a strong metaphor for the dehydration of man's liveliness :

The ardour
With which I bled the stoic pride
Of the existentialist
Has dried up even the harsh
Sunlight of my Indian sky.

One may easily see the contrast between Rajasekharaiah's approach and that of Vedic seers. Whereas the Vedic seers worshipped the Indian sun as source of all life and energy, Rajasekharaiah is compelled to see the same Indian sun as a deccicator of all life and energy :

Faith is not supported by any direct personal experience for the poet who feels that it is just a family gift :

That faith
Was a warm rug for the inevitable
Evening cold,
A parental gift, part of the family

Goods
And no more.

Life has become a big folly and utterly meaningless for the poet and his like :

Both words
And wordlessness have
Given the lie to truth.

That is the reason why the poet feels like escaping from India to a foreign land. He further points out the supremacy of evil over good in India through the mythological imagery :

The Menakas
And Rambhas of the land
Are there
Assigned by the jealous gods
To wean away the Viswamitras
From a knowledge that is not
For man.

Evil is so powerful that it does not allow the free play of good in India. The poet further says that Indians are always bothered about the satisfaction of animal needs and the higher things like spiritual or scientific knowledge turn out to be simply irrelevant for them :

What profits the wisdom
Of Christ or Einstein
For a cup whose primal need is
Protein and the vitamins
And a little animal ease
For the burden of the glands?

The poet's bitterness may be seen in his awareness of the overwhelming meaninglessness of life in India :

And fond
Was the enthronement owing
Allegiance
To an emptiness enshrined in an
Emptiness.

In spite of all high spiritual speculations about heaven and renunciation, the Indians are dragged powerfully back to the earthly and sensuous life. The poet suggests how Mature triumphs over culture and ties man in the net of *maya* :

> When we call ourselves masters
> Of all that is here,
> Viceroys
> Of an emperor in a distant heaven,
> The earth laughs,
> For a whore's voluptuous antics
> Vibrate the world
> Into sound, motion and form
> To suck them in.

Thus ultimately the poet is disillusioned by his shocking awareness of the triumph of opportunism over idealism; ignorance over knowledge and sensuousness over spirituality. The poem begins and end on a note of pessimism.

Rajasekharaiah's disappointment with the harsh reality of Indian life is reflected in "The Urgent Need." The poet does not want to bother about heaven or the so-called future. His main concern is with the present. His main desire is to lead a comfortable life of material pleasure and satisfaction :

> Not heaven of the cloudless grace,
> Nor that tiny warm place
> In the memory of tomorrow :
> They are not urgent.

What is urgent for the poet is to have a comfortable day-to-day life without the unnecessary struggle. He, therefore, says :

> Give me the language to buy the ticket
> Before the train leaves; the special phrase
> Which gets the unadulterated milk,
> The right quantity of sugar
> Without the queue and the black rate
> Rice not enriched with the unnourishing pebble,
> Coffee or tea that is coffee or tea,
> The pen that writes, the car that moves,
> The road that reaches the terminal,
> Words which bring me all these
> Without the special fee.

The bite of these lines can be understood only by those who know the harsh realities of Indian life. A foreign reader, for example, an American or a Canadian or a Britisher cannot easily visualise these dire conditions of Indian existence. In India, a sensitive man has to face problems almost at every step, because of corruption, adulteration, moral degeneration and overcrowdedness of life. Such a vision is easily corroborated by V.S. Naipaul in his *Overcrowded Barracoon.*

Likewise, the poet wants to get a full seat for himself in the bus which is generally overcrowded; live in peace without being disturbed by senseless blare of the neighbour's radio and not to listen to the vulgar language of uncultured people. Similarly he wants to be free from the foul smell of his fellow creatures who might care more for holiness than for hygienic cleanliness. He wishes to buy goods in the market without the mediation of brokers ('the brokering rats') and does not want his goodness to mistaken "for the buyer's ignorance/Meant by all the earthly ways/To enhance/The efficacy of the market place."

Rajasekharaiah's prayer picturises the Indian society which is inflicted with moral ugliness and corruption so vehemently attacked by other sensitive writers like Nirad Chaudhuri and V.S. Naipaul among others. His prayer brings to our mind similar prayers by Basaveswara (12th century mystic poet from Karnataka) and by Mahatma Gandhi uttered in almost similar situations.

Finally the poet makes it very clear that the earthly life is more important than the so-called heaven which can perhaps be experienced in sleep or dream or memory. His only ambition is to live the this worldly life happily :

> Give me the will and the power
> For the earth;
> For that heaven
> I have enough in one sleepy gesture
> Of my soul.

Rajasekharaiah's sense of irritation is articulated in "Gods and Apes" where the poet wonders at the simian bliss as compared to the sensitive human being. It is said that it is foolish to be wise among fools. The same philosophy is expressed in paradoxical terms by the poet who says :

> There is no grief more grievous
> Than a sensitive soul.

The sensitive soul is bound to suffer on account of its sensitiveness whereas the mindless beings like animals seem to be blissfully content with their mindlessness, non-interrogation and acceptance of the contingencies of life. The poet illustrates his general paradoxical observation with a couple of bovine and canine metaphors :

> Give me the buffalo chewing cud,
> The earthen being,
> Rolling a little earth in the tongue
> Satiated or the bone chewing dog
> Master of all food.

Then the poet offers another paradoxical observation which is applicable to all aristocratic minds including the poet's :

> But nothing is poorer than a rich mind,
> A wealthy soul.

Such a rich mind and wealthy soul is compelled by the contingencies of life to lead a very poor materialistic life :

> Regal taste reduced to frugal table,
> The poor pittance
> The parsimonious flesh yields.

Disappointed with an impecunious life, the poet longs to be one of the mindless creatures of the world for whom all peace and plenty is promised :

> O to be a beast
> Or the little grain among seas
> Of sand, or ant
> Or the unmetaphysical bird,
> Darlings of earth!

The longing to belong to the mass of anonymous creatures in propelled by the pessimistic realisation that

> Woe is a god among snoring apes.

The poem, thus, not only shows paradoxically the bitterness of the sensitive poet, but also betrays his own egoistic superiority and separatism. The overall philosophy of the poet is parallel to Wordsworth's and Gray's though the manner of expression is quite different from their's.

Rajasekharaiah, like other sensitive writers like Nirad Chaudhuri and V.S. Naipaul, has noticed the Indian lethargy caused by the tropical sun of India. There is something deterministic about the horrible climate affecting the Indians adversely. He describes it in "The Tropical Jungle" thus :

> A red sun and a bronze sky
> Mould our shape.

Then he points out how the horrid sun kills the beauty of human personality and dehydrates all the warmth of his heart and incapacitates him for any aesthetic enjoyment of life :

> Flowers in us burn and droop.
> Bent, we retire into the dark silent cell
> And have no wakefulness for the moon.
> Winter sports on the vital snows,
> Invitations to joy,
> Those have passed the other way.

The Indian is trapped in the tropical climate where he can neither face the horrid sun nor enjoy the pleasant moon nor dream of winter sports on the snow. In spite of abundant light around him, he is driven into the dark world which can be both physical and spiritual. The poet continues further to show dehumanising effect of the horrible on the Indian mind and his consequent helplessness :

> Nothing stirs the hidden birds,
> An amazing fire
> Pours herbal peace
> To all sorrowings.
> None, not one of those things
> That water the soul
> For thought or dream
> Neither motion

Nor emotion
One infinite midday drowsiness
From outside
And from inside
Hugs the tropical wilderness,
Life slumbers
Under an original spell.

Thus India emerges as a country where no creativity is possible because of the tropical sun.

In "The Liliputians" Rajasekharaiah highlights the contrast between technological advancement and expansion on the one hand and moral retrogression and diminution on the other. The poet's satire and anger are symbolically concretised in the very appellation he gives to the people of the modern world. These liliputians who are morally dwarf are universally distributed and recognised as they have extra-ordinary powers of controlling the universe :

The liliputians have a field day,
Dale and hill and widespread field,
Their tents are pitched. The deed
Are registered, promulgated, advertising
For world knowledge.
Their undisputed possession
Of so much land, acre by acre,
Boundaries clarified by an account
Of the ocean on the western coast
Flowing around the southern cape
To join the eastern one.

Although the liliputians are very small in their physical and moral stature, they are very powerful in their capacity for acquisition, encroachment and expansion. They are the great conquerors of the world, with all the political, bureaucratic and military power. The poet expresses it in the following lines :

Their agents
Are on the trespassing waters
From the shores, their sentinels,
Each in his cubicle, musket

And wand and the forbidding board
Keeping walkers off under threat
Of possession.

Because of their authoritarianism, they can suppress or destroy the natural beauty of the world :

Grass and flower
And fruity tree, cowed and silenced,
Withdraw beyond the broadening fence
And seek refuge in the sea.

Although morally dwarfish, the liliputians are capable of using the amenities of modern technology (perhaps even science) to erect skyscrapers tall enough to reach the sky and wide enough to cover the boundaries of the earth :

Cement and concrete, steel and glass,
Rise up from the earth,
Reach to the sky in chains
Of marching smoke. From within
The giant hills push out lines
Of manufactured midgets of steel limb,
Cement flesh, concrete skin and glass mind
To people the wide open spaces
Of immensely empty universe
From which life and the joy of life have fled.

The paradox happens to be that the liliputians try to cover up their lack of moral power by possession of official or political power; their moral stodgyness by their inhabitance in sky-kissing mansions; their own moral and aesthetic emptiness by filling the empty universe with the expansion of their own population.

The poem is seriously satirical in its tone and universal in its applicability, as it is not confined only to India, but extends over to the entire world. It is the small man who rules the world by wielding his authority from an elevated seat. The pessimistic note of the poem cannot be questioned by any sensible man.

Rajasekharaiah's satirical attack on the good luck of the ignorant and the bad luck of the intelligent may be seen in his "Mother Earth." The first part of the poem shows the relative unimportance of man in the world because of the presence of a diversity of other things and beings. He declares that

> The earth is not the particular
> Palace of man.

He then shows the contrast between the suffering of man and the enjoyment of the non-human beings :

> Where the humans starve,
> The roach, the termite, the rat flourish;
> The white ant reigns emperor. Organic,
> Inorganic, all substance yields him tribute.

The poet thus deplores the supremacy of non-human being over the human beings. He shows his sadness and anger through the interrogation :

> Is man with his politics the darling
> Child of Nature?

Then he proves his point by declaring that :

> She loves the brute,
> Her most milk for the mindless brat,
> Crawling and dependent.

In the second half of the poem, the metaphor of 'mother' is shifted from the cosmic world to the human world; from the earth to woman. Yet a parallel is seen between the earth and the mother. The mother who is growing more and more insecure on account of her advancing years, fears of the gradual loss of her power over her own intelligent and academic son :

> The ageing mother
> Who in secret fear the academic son
> And hates her established sway menaced
> By his independent love with her own
> Different foreign ways.

Finally the poet shows the paradox of life by showing the transformation of embracing love into rejecting fear :

> The cradle that
> Rocked the infant to sleep ejects the adult.

At a deeper level, the poet discerns a sort of power-politics not only in the cosmos, but also in the human world. The mother is safe only when her son is a baby in the cradle and becomes insecure when the baby grows into an adult. The cradle, thus, becomes a symbol for maternal power and security.

In "The Collective Man" Rajasekharaiah satirically highlights the contrast between individuality and collectiveness; between class and mass and laments the suppression of individual light and beauty in the face of mass culture and statistical quantity. The mass culture enjoys the power of its mass :

> The collective man is a fool
> And a tyrant,
> He rules the world.
> God's men are single
> And alone.
> The power once theirs
> Has not survived
> The change of order, only
> The species surviving.

The poet shows how the world has no place for recognition of individual life, beauty and achievement. It is only the mindless beings (like animals) and entities who survive in the competitive world or cosmos :

> Fittest
> To survive are ants, cocroaches,
> Locusts and rodents,
> Nations, parties and governments.

Then the poet proceeds to point out the paradoxical nature of the world which tries to honour or glorify the very individuals whom it has destroyed :

> The lone lights are shifted
> In their own sockets, starved
> Or felled like the tall single giants
> Rising to the skies
> Or the earth dries up at the roots,
> Later giving them a place
> Among the stars
> Or a name among angels
> Comprising empty labels
> After burning the mortal limbs.

The poet satirises the suppression of individuality by the mass culture or mobocracy or collective culture and the meaningless celebration of the same principle by the latter. One might easily see an attack on communism and conformism in this short poem from an individualistic perspective.

Rajasekharaiah's satirical attack is directed to the academic life in "Diploma in English Speech." Foreign returned Indian scholars trained in British pronunciation, syntax and usage develop a snobbish up-in-the-air attitude and look down upon the literary scholars. These linguists and phoneticians, in spite of their slavish imitations of British masters, consider themselves as a privileged class and labour under the illusion that it is only they who can wield the alien language correctly and precisely and not the others. They do not know that they reduce the language to a dead mechanicity by forgetting and forsaking the imaginative, creative and dynamic aspect of language. Irritated by the artificial atmosphere of arrogance aired by Indian linguists and especially phoneticians, Rajasekharaiah bursts out metaphorically :

> Words upon a time were magic spells
> That drew a rabbit from the hat;
> Now they've become electric bells
> That tickle the ears of the cat.

The poet's satirical attack on the failure of language (in the hands of linguists) to awaken the creative powers of man and its reduction to the mundane function of attracting a mindless animal is evident here. The poet continues his attack :

> Once with them the human mind
> The Persian carpet rode;
> But now they are well devised
> Like milestones along the road.

The poet metaphorically shows the contrast between the imaginative use of language and the mechanical use of the same. The language used by imaginative people is as picturesque, colourful and rich as a Persian carpet, but the one used by the modern linguists is notorious for its dead and mechanical uniformity comparable to milestones along the road. The contrast is continued in the next stanza :

Once they baited the earth and sky,
The sun and the moon and stars;
Now they are the tuppenny, hapenny
Exchangeable for candybars.

The language of the imaginative helps them enter into communion with cosmic forces whereas the language of modern linguists can be used only as a currency for buying trivial things. The same satirical contrast may be found in the last stanza :

One little word had once us led
To fairies, angels and Gods;
The Gods are dead, the fairies are fled,
For the D.E.S. wields the roads.

Once language happened to be a means of communication with Gods and other ethereal beings, whereas now it has unfortunately become a medium handled by the diploma-holders for communication in a Godless and mundane and mechanical world. The poem is a fine satire on the snobbish products of the Central Institute of English who are alienated from the Indian context and who reproduce foreign theories like parrots without caring for their applicability to the Indian multicultural and multilingual situation.

An attempt has been made in this article to introduce a sample of T.R. Rajasekharaiah's satirical poetry. His other kinds of poetry like the reflective, philosophical, and humorous poetry have yet to be examined by the Indian English critics. On the whole, Rajasekharaiah's poetry is known for its serious tone and wry humour. It can easily be compared and contrasted with that of other serious poets of India like Nissim Ezekiel, Keki Daruwalla, Shiva K. Kumar and Jayanta Mahapatra. His poetry provides a fertile ground for research students for M.Phil., and even Ph.D. degrees.

CONTRIBUTORS

Basavaraj Naikar, Professor and Chairman, Department of English, Karnataka University, Dharwad, Karnataka.

Binod Mishra, B.I.T.S., Pilani, Rajasthan.

Ramesh Kumar Gupta, Chapra (Saran), Bihar.

G.A. Ghanshyam, Assistant Professor of English, Government Auto. Science P.G. College, Bilaspur, Chhattisgarh.

Shankar Prasad Singha, Reader in English, Vidyasagar University, Midnapore, West Bengal.

Aroonima Sinha, Lecturer in English, C.M. College, Darbhanga, Bihar.

P.D. Dubbe, Reader in English, Yeshwant Mahavidyalaya, Nanded, Maharashtra.

Asha Choubey, Lecturer in English, Kanya Mahavidyalaya, Bareilly, Uttar Pradesh.

S.N. Vikram Raj Urs, Professor of English, Karnataka State Open University, Manasa Gangotri, Mysore, Karnataka.

N.B. Masal, Department of English, Dr. Ghali College, Gadhinglaj, District : Kolhapur, Maharashtra.

Kuldeep Kumar, Department of English, N.P.G. College, Shikohabad, Uttar Pradesh.

Gajendra Kumar, Department of English Studies and Research, Agra College, Agra, Uttar Pradesh.

Mukesh Ranjan Verma, Professor & Head, Department of English, Gurukul Kangri University, Haridwar, Uttaranchal.

M.A. Nare, Lecturer in English, Government P.G. College, Amaravati, Maharashtra.